THE ISLAMIST PHOENIX

THE ISLAMIST PHOENIX

THE ISLAMIC STATE (ISIS) AND THE
REDRAWING OF THE MIDDLE EAST

LORETTA NAPOLEONI

Seven Stories Press
New York / Oakland

A Seven Stories Press First Edition

Seven Stories Press
140 Watts Street
New York, NY 10013
www.sevenstories.com

College professors and high school and middle school teachers may order free examination copies of Seven Stories Press titles. To order, visit http://www.sevenstories.com/contact or send a fax on school letterhead to (212) 226-1411.

Book design by Jon Gilbert

Library of Congress Cataloging-in-Publication Data

Napoleoni, Loretta.
  The Islamist phoenix : Islamic State and the redrawing of the Middle East / Loretta Napoleoni.
     pages cm
  ISBN 978-1-60980-628-6 (pbk.)
  1. IS (Organization) 2. Middle East--History--21st century. 3. Islamic fundamentalism--21st century. 4. Terrorism--Middle East. I. Title.
  HV6433.I722I8563 2014
  956.05'4--dc23

                                 2014038288

Printed in the United States

9 8 7 6 5 4 3 2

To Giuseppe
Thank you for your support

CONTENTS

CONTENTS

NOTE ON TERMINOLOGY

The rise to power of the armed organization that in June 2014 took the name Islamic State has been swift and, until recently, largely undetected. In recent years this group has frequently changed its name. Originally part of Abu Mussab al Zarqawi's organization *Tawhid al Jihad*, it later became the Islamist State in Iraq (ISI), which eventually merged into al Qaeda in Iraq. In 2010, when Abu Bakr al Baghdadi became its leader, the group reverted to its former appellation the Islamic State in Iraq. In 2013, following its merger with a section of *Jabhat al Nusra*, a Syrian jihadist group affiliated with al Qaeda, the organization renamed itself Islamic State in Iraq and the Levant (al Sham), better known by the acronym ISIL or ISIS.[1] Finally, just before the declaration of the Caliphate, ISIS became the Islamic State. In Syria, however, right from the beginning, and today in Iraq also, the group has been known simply *al Dawlat*, the State.

Each new term corresponds with major developments and important changes in the life of the organization. As such, the semantics of the Islamic State constitute one additional piece of the Middle Eastern political puzzle that the West and the world are trying to put together.

The name *al Tawhid al Jihad*, often translated as Monotheism and Jihad, conveys a sense that God is everything and everywhere; life can exist only within His rule. Accordingly, Muslims consider the original Islamic State, the first Caliphate, the seventh-century creation of the Prophet Mohammed and his companions, a perfect society ruled by divine mandate. In short, it was the political expression of the will of God. Today, the trademark gesture of al Tawhid, the thrusting of one's index finger to the sky, has become the all but official salute of the contemporary Islamic State.

The transition from al Tawhid al Jihad to the Islamic State in Iraq coincided with the efforts of al Zarqawi's armed group to focus on Iraq, to confine its jihad to this country, as a launching pad to re-establish the Caliphate. In similar fashion, al Baghdadi's decision to add the words "al Sham," the ancient Arabic denomination of Damascus and surrounding territories, from which some of the first Caliphs ruled, represents a step forward from his predecessor and marks the beginning of a cross-border effort to achieve the organization's final goal: the reconstruction of the Caliphate.

The birth of the Islamic State, the newest name taken by ISIS, just a day before the declaration of the establishment of the Caliphate, signifies a major new stage of nation-building, the process of recreating the circumstances that in the seventh century led to the establishment of Islam's ideal society.

Today, Western media and politicians use various designations to describe the armed organization led by al Baghdadi. The White House and Downing Street use ISIL, while the US media prefers ISIS. PBS, however, favors the Islamic State, while some in the Australian media have adopted the terminology Islamic State Group, to avoid giving the impression that it is a state instead of an armed organization. Overall in English, the acronymic ISIS and ISIL sound better than IS, hence their popularity. The reluctance of politicians to use the word "state" springs from the fear of accepting, if only with a word, the claim of the Islamic State to be not a terrorist organization, but a state legitimized by a war of conquest and internal consensus.

In the course of this book I have used the term Islamic State because this is how the group has most recently defined itself and likely how it will continue to be known. It is my opinion that the term Islamic State carries a much more realistic message to the world than does ISIS or ISIL. This message conveys the group's determination to succeed at building the twenty-first-century version of the Caliphate. Using less precise acronyms for propaganda reasons, for example, to hide the true nature of the Islamic State, will not help us face the current threat. On the contrary, it will most likely, yet again, prevent us from developing an ad hoc strategy to bring peace once and for all to the Middle East.

INTRODUCTION

For the first time since World War I, an armed organization is redesigning the map of the Middle East drawn by the French and the British. Waging a war of conquest, the Islamic State (IS), formerly known as the Islamic State of Iraq and the Levant (al Sham), ISIL or ISIS, is erasing the borders that the Sykes-Picot Accord established in 1916. Today the black and gold flag of IS flies across a territory larger than the United Kingdom or Texas, from the Mediterranean shores of Syria well into the heart of Iraq, the Sunni tribal area. Since late June 2014, this region has been known as the Islamic Caliphate,[2] a designation that had previously ceased to exist with the dissolution of the Ottoman Empire at the hands of Ataturk in 1924.

In the Islamic State, as in al Qaeda before it, many Western observers see an anachronistic organization that seeks to turn back the clock. Indeed Syrian and Iraqi refugees have described its rule as indistinguishable from that of the Taliban regime. Posters forbid smoking and the use of cameras; women are not allowed to travel without a male relative; they must be covered up and cannot wear trousers in public.[3] At the same time, the Islamic State seems engaged in a sort of religious cleansing through aggressive proselytization. Residents of its territory who do not flee must adopt its radical Salafist creed or face execution.

Since his ascent to the global stage, IS leader and Caliph Abu Bakr al Baghdadi has drawn comparisons to al Qaeda's Mullah Omar. Ironically, these comparisons may well have led Western intelligence to underestimate him and his organization's strength. Despite its seemingly medieval approach to legality and social control, to deem the IS essentially backward would be mistaken. While the world of the Taliban was limited to Koranic schools and knowledge based upon the writings of the Prophet, globalization and modern technology have been the incubator of the Islamic State.

What distinguishes this organization from all other armed groups that predate it—including those active during the Cold War—and what accounts for its enormous successes is its modernity[4] and pragmatism. Its leadership shows an unparalleled grasp of the limitations facing contemporary powers in a globalized and multipolar world. For example, IS sensed, before most others had, that joint foreign intervention of the sort that occurred in Libya and Iraq would not be possible in Syria. Against this backdrop, the Islamic State's leadership has successfully exploited to its own advantage, and almost unobserved, the Syrian conflict—a contemporary version of the traditional war-by-proxy with plenty of sponsors and armed groups. Seeking a regime change in Syria, the Kuwaitis, Qataris, and Saudis have been willing to bankroll a plethora of armed organizations, of which IS is only one. However, instead of fighting its sponsors' war by proxy, the Islamic State has used their money to establish its own territorial strongholds in financially strategic regions, like the rich oilfields of Eastern Syria. No previous Middle Eastern armed organization has been able to promote itself as the region's new ruler using the money of its rich Gulf sponsors.

In sharp contrast with the Taliban's rhetoric, and despite its barbarous treatment of its enemies, the Islamic State is spreading a powerful, in part positive, political message in the Muslim world: the return of the Caliphate, a new Golden Age of Islam. This message comes at a time of great destabilization in the Middle East, with Syria and Iraq ablaze, Libya on the verge of another tribal conflict, Egypt restive and ruled by the army, and Israel once again at war with Gaza. Hence, the rebirth of the Caliphate under its new Caliph, al Baghdadi, appears to many Sunnis not as the emergence of yet another armed group but as the rise of a promising new political entity from the ashes of decades of war and destruction.

The fact that this Islamist Phoenix materialized on the first day of Ramadan 2014, the holy month of fasting and prayer, should be regarded as a powerful omen of the challenge that the Islamic State poses to the legitimacy of all fifty-seven countries whose citizens predominantly follow the Islamic faith. As IS spokesman Abu Mohammed al Adnani has put it: "the legality of all emirates, groups, states, and organizations becomes null by the expansion of the Caliph's authority and the arrival of his troops in their areas." It is a challenge posed by a contemporary state commanding a modern army, which traces its legitimacy to the first territorial manifestation of Islam in seventh- and eighth-century Arabia.

This very real threat is particularly felt by those who share a border with Syria and Iraq. In July 2014 the flag of the Islamic State appeared in Jordanian villages, and in August thousands of IS militants streamed into Lebanon from Syria, taking the town of Arsal. Since this offensive was launched, even former sponsors now fear the military power of the Caliphate: at the beginning of July, Saudi Arabia deployed 30,000 soldiers to its border with Iraq after the Iraqi army withdrew from the area.

Beneath the religious veneer and the terrorist tactics, however, lies a political and military machine fully engaged in nation-building, and, more surprisingly, in seeking consensus in the wake of its territorial conquests. Residents of the enclaves that the Caliphate controls affirm that the arrival of IS fighters coincided with improvements in the day-to-day running of their villages. IS fighters fixed potholes, organized soup kitchens for those who had lost their homes, and secured round-the-clock electricity.[5] In so doing, IS exhibits some understanding that in the twenty-first century, new nations cannot be built by terror and violence alone. To succeed, they require popular consensus.

While territorially the master plan is to recreate the ancient Caliphate of Baghdad—an entity that stretched from the Iraqi capital all the way into modern Israel in its heyday, before being destroyed by the Mongols in 1258—politically the goal of the Islamic State is to craft its twenty-first-century incarnation. In his first speech as the new Caliph, al Baghdadi pledged to return to Muslims the "dignity, might, rights, and leadership" of the past and called for doctors, engineers, judges, and experts in Islamic jurisprudence to join him.[6] As he spoke, a team of translators across the world worked to release, almost in real time, the text of his speech on jihadist websites, and on Facebook and Twitter accounts, in several languages including English, French, and German.[7]

To many, the Islamic State's main aim is to be for Sunni Muslims what Israel is for Jews: a state in their ancient land, reclaimed in modern times; a powerful religious state that protects them wherever they are. For how shocking and repugnant this comparison is, it is nonetheless the potent message broadcast to the disenfranchised Muslim youth who live in the political vacuum created by disturbing factors such as the rampant corruption, inequality, and injustice of modern Muslim states; the ruthless dictatorship of Bashar al Assad; the Nouri al Maliki government's refusal to integrate Sunnis into the fabric of Iraqi political life and end their persecution by the Baghdad political machine; the failure to replace the socio-economic infrastructure destroyed during the war; and the high rate of unemployment. It is a powerful and, at the same time, seductive message also for those living abroad, the disenfranchised European and American Muslim youth who struggle to integrate in a Western society that offers fewer and fewer opportunities to young generations. No other armed organization has shown such insight into, and political intuition regarding, the domestic politics of the Middle East and Muslim immigrants' frustration all over the world. No other armed organization has so successfully adapted to contingent factors, such as the provision of basic socio-economic infrastructure and business partnership with local authorities in the territory it controls, in its efforts at nation-building.

Indeed, the leadership of IS has studied the tactics and structure of other armed groups, and has applied these lessons in a new context. Like the European armed organizations of the 1960s and 1970s, such as the Red Brigades in Italy and the IRA in Northern Ireland, the Islamic State appreciates the power of the "propaganda of fear," and has been especially skilled at using social media to propagate sleek videos and images of its barbarous actions to local and global audiences. That fear is a much more potent weapon of conquest than religious lectures is a fact that al Qaeda failed to understand. Equally, the Islamic State appreciates that extreme violence sells the news: in a world overloaded with information, the twenty-four-hour media cycle seeks ever more graphic images—thus the surfeit of photos and videos of brutal punishments and tortures uploaded in formats that can be easily watched on mobile phones. In our voyeuristic, virtual society, appealingly packaging what appears to be sadism has become a great show.

IS has also drawn lessons in the power of propaganda from closer to home. The Islamic State has analyzed the propaganda machines that the US and UK administrations employed to justify their preventive strike on Iraq in 2003. It has paid particular attention to the February 5, 2003, UN Security Council speech by then-US Secretary of State Colin Powell, credited with creating the myth of Abu Mussad al Zarqawi to justify the invasion of Iraq. Thanks to an extensive and highly professional use of social media, the Islamic State has generated equally false mythologies to proselytize, recruit, and raise funds across the Muslim world.

Crucial to the success of this strategy has been the web of secrecy and mythology carefully woven around IS leader Abu Bakr al Baghdadi. In this information-saturated world, mystery also plays a major role in stimulating the collective imagination. The more something is concealed, the more one desires it to be revealed, and the less one knows, the more one imagines. Offer viewers a few clips, and they will complete the picture as they like it. Modern advertising has constructed a trillion-dollar industry upon these simple concepts. Now the Islamic State's propaganda machine is using them to manufacture the myth of al Baghdadi and of the new Caliphate. Islam is premised on the mystery of the return of the Prophet. Hence, at the same time that IS terrorizes Westerners with shockingly barbarous killings, it leads Muslim supporters to believe that the Prophet has returned in the clothes of al Baghdadi. What's surprising is our surprise.

Using the stick of violence and Sharia law along with the carrot of propagandistic social media and a variety of popular social programs aimed at improving the living conditions of the Sunni population trapped inside the Caliphate, IS shows its deep pragmatism. (In this regard too, it is distinguished from al Qaeda.) If this strategy succeeds, the international community will be forced to confront a new scenario in the history of terrorism and nation-building. That is, the Islamic State will have provided a workable solution to the "dilemma of terrorism," which is the ultimate challenge for the modern state.

Indeed, the modern state must decide whether to consider acts of terrorism a threat to national security or to law and order. This dilemma springs from the double responsibility of the modern state: to protect its citizens from outside enemies and from domestic criminals. Armed groups want to overthrow existing states, so they pose a threat to national security; for example IS's goal is to free the territories of the old Caliphate of Baghdad from the tyrannical rule of the Shiites and to annex Jordan and Israel to recreate such an entity. However, armed groups use criminal, and in the case of al Qaeda or the Islamic State, barbarous means, such as suicide bombings and even the crucifixion of opponents to achieve their goals. Until Bush's war on terror, states had dismissed terrorism as a form of crime, i.e., a threat to law and order, and used their judiciaries to deal with it. Even when Bush declared that al Qaeda was a menace to national security, its members were considered unlawful combatants and never granted the status of enemies. Terrorism, therefore, could be defined as a crime with the aims of war.[8]

However, if the Islamic State, using the means of terrorism to gain territorial control and social and political reforms to secure popular consensus, prevails in building a modern state, one with which the world must reckon, it will have proven what all armed organizations have professed: that its members are not criminals but enemies engaged in an asymmetrical war to overthrow illegitimate, tyrannical, and corrupted regimes.

This book has been written while the Islamic State's war of conquest progresses, keeping close track of current news. As this conflict will continue for quite some time, the book attempts to answer key questions about the nature and goals of the Islamic State and the Caliphate, not to predict the outcome of such conflict, but to help the reader understand its true nature. One conclusion that we can immediately draw is that since 9/11 the business of Islamist terrorism has been getting stronger not weaker—to the extent that it has now expanded into the field of nation-building—by simply keeping abreast of a fast-changing world in which propaganda and technology play an increasingly vital role. The same cannot be said for the forces engaged in stopping it from spreading.

A New Breed of Terrorism?

During the last three years, the Islamic State's successes have been unprecedented. By brutal means and steely insight it may achieve the historically unachievable: the reconstruction of the Caliphate. In the post–World War II period, no armed group has ever carved out such a large territory. At its height, the PLO, by far the largest armed organization in the Middle East, controlled only a fraction of the land that the Islamic State rules today. This accomplishment is often attributed to the Syrian conflict, which is seen as the incubator of a new breed of terrorism.

Indeed, in the throes of a post–Arab Spring civil war, and rife with its own insurgent Islamists, Syria provides a convenient narrative to foreclose any thought of a common thread linking the Islamic State to 9/11 and the 2003 US invasion of Iraq. The West and the world desperately cling to the idea that the horrifying present of Iraq and Syria has no historical precedent, that we are not responsible for current events in the Middle East. Hence, in contrast with the rugged forces of al Qaeda in Afghanistan or the suicide army of al Zarqawi in Iraq, the

Islamic State is depicted as a new species: an organization able to generate vast income, acting as a multinational of violence, commanding a large and modern army, and bankrolling fully trained soldiers. All this is true. What is not is the novelty and uniqueness of its genetic traits.

Certainly, unlike the Taliban or al Qaeda, the Islamic State manages vast revenues, generated in part through the annexation of productive assets, such as oil fields and electrical power stations across Syria. According to the *Wall Street Journal*, the export of oil alone generates $2 million per day.[9] In addition, inside the territory it controls, it levies taxes on businesses as well as on sales of arms, other military equipment, and general goods, most of them in transit across lucrative smuggling routes along Syria's borders with Turkey and Iraq. The exceptional "business acumen" of this organization vis-à-vis not only the Taliban, but all other armed groups, was recently confirmed by the accidental discovery of its "annual report." Setting out a detailed account of revenues and expenses, down to the cost of each suicide mission, and compiled according to the most sophisticated accounting techniques, the report shows what a reader would be forgiven for mistaking as the budget of a thriving, legitimate multinational.[10]

The Islamic State's ability to function as a corporation of terror, however, is not unique—neither is its capacity to generate monetary wealth, nor its understanding of the importance of strategic assets, such as the Mosul Dam.

By the mid-1990s, according to the CIA, the PLO had accumulated between \$8 and \$14 billion, a figure higher than the then-GDP of Bahrain (\$6 billion), Jordan (\$10.6 billion), and Yemen (\$6.5 billion).[11] With an estimated wealth of \$2 billion, the Islamic State has a long way to go to match the wealth of the PLO.[12]

Where IS does outmatch past armed organizations is in military prowess, media manipulation, social programs, and, above all, nation-building. These subtle advantages in the programs traditionally undertaken by armed groups suggest an improvement on the old model of terrorism, not a genetic mutation. Indeed, these enhancements spring from the ability of the Islamic State to adapt to a fast changing, post–Cold War environment.

In the past, terrorist activity was confined inside small territories held by powerful states' armies: the PLO battled the Israeli military machine, the IRA, the British army. Equally, the territorial aspirations of insurgent organizations were necessarily limited by larger Cold War alliances that shored up state borders, while only the two superpowers could afford to fund wars-by-proxy.

Today, we operate in a multipolar world of changing alliances, rife with state sponsorship of terrorism. Hence the Islamic State has been able to carve out its Caliphate inside a vast region plagued by sectarian wars and funded by several state sponsors. In so doing it has been facing more than one enemy—the Syrian and Iraqi armies, the Islamic Front, a coalition of Jihadist groups, the Syrian rebels, as well as the Shiite militias and the Kurdish Pesh-merga—all engaged on multiple fronts, some weakened by corruption.[13] This distinction is key and explains how the Islamic State has succeeded in waging a war of conquest that threatens to rupture the modern borders of so large an area as the entire Middle East, something that no armed organization has achieved before.

If its economic and military prowess has not distinguished it as a new breed of terrorism, neither has its penchant for pre-modern displays of barbarous violence, which Western media have incorrectly reported as a shock even to the leadership of al Qaeda. It was al Qaeda itself whose infamous 9/11 mastermind Khalid Sheikh Mohammed was responsible for the 2002 beheading of *Wall Street Journal* reporter Daniel Pearl, an act which, for the first time, broadcast to the world this type of barbaric murder. Pearl's execution was followed, in 2004, by the beheading of Nicholas Berg at the hands of Abu Musab al Zarqawi's group. The same year, the ambush of four Blackwater contractors, whose burning bodies were dragged through the street of Fallujah, represented what many had thought was the nadir of evil. Sadly, the violent acts of the Islamic State are not without equal.

From the ashes of the War on Terror, therefore, in a post–Cold War proxy environment, the Islamic State has repackaged itself not as a new breed of terrorism but as a mutation of its former self. Its success springs from the convergence of several factors, among which are a globalized multipolar world, a command of modern technology, a pragmatic attempt at nation-building, a deep understanding of the psychology of Middle Eastern and Muslim emigrants, and the long shadow of the West's response to 9/11, which has plunged parts of the Middle East into a decade of sectarian warfare. Ignoring these facts is more than misleading and superficial, it is dangerous. "Know your enemy" remains the most important adage in the fight against terrorism.

Chapter One

From al Zarqawi to al Baghdadi

The success of the Islamic State forces us to a moment of reckoning. It is time to declare the failure of counter-terrorism to prevent the advent of the Caliphate, and it is time to face our responsibilities. The world is in need of a new approach to stopping this hostile political entity, especially now as it redraws, in blood, the borders of the Middle East. Such a strategy cannot be produced by denying the obvious fact that the genesis of the Caliphate is deeply intertwined with decades of Western politics and interventions in the Middle East.

If IS succeeds in building one nation across Iraq and Syria, the threat posed by this achievement will go well beyond the political landscape of these two nations. For the first time in modern history, an armed organization will have fulfilled the final goal of terrorism: to create its own state on the ashes of existing nations, not through a revolution, as happened in Iran, but through a traditional war of conquest based upon terrorist tactics.[14] If it does so, the Islamic State will have become the new model of terrorism.

How did we get to this point? The long answer must be sought in the post-war partition of the Middle East at the hands of the former colonial powers. The short answer is found in the confluence of the preventive strike in Iraq and the civil war in Syria. The former created one of modern jihad's most brilliant and enigmatic strategists, the late Abu Musab al Zarqawi, a man who openly challenged the historical leadership of al Qaeda and who, as we shall see, reignited the ancient and bloody conflict between Sunnis and Shiites as a key tactic for the rebirth of the Caliphate. Syria provided a unique opportunity, a launch pad, for those who had assimilated al Zarqawi's message and who wished to achieve his dream, among them Abu Bakr al Baghdadi, the new Caliph.[15]

To understand how in the space of a decade a group of jihadists became a rogue force capable of destabilizing entire regions and exposing their deepest political and sectarian contradictions, one needs to step back in time, to the rising star of al Zarqawi and the outbreak of the Syrian conflict.

The Legacy of al Zarqawi

Of Bedouin origins, Abu Musab al Zarqawi was born in a working-class section of Zarqa, Jordan's second-largest city, just seven months before the start of the Six-Day War in 1967. A troubled youth and petty criminal, in his early twenties he was arrested and spent five years in prison, where he embraced radical Salafism, a doctrine that, as we shall see, calls for a total rejection of Western values and influence. Still today, Salafism is the creed embraced by the Islamic State. On al Zarqawi's release, he immediately left for Afghanistan to join the Mujahidin, but arrived too late to fight the Soviets.

In 2000, in Kandahar, Afghanistan, al Zarqawi met Osama bin Laden for the first time. Boldly, the young jihadist rejected the Saudi's invitation to become part of al Qaeda. Al Zarqawi was not prepared to fight against the US, the far away enemy. Instead, he wanted to wage his struggle against the near enemy, the Jordanian government, and establish a truly Islamic state in the region. This became the purpose of the modest training camp that he was soon operating in Herat, Afghanistan, near the Iranian border, preparing suicide bombers for missions across the Middle East.

Indeed, al Zarqawi's entry into the Iraqi arena was marked by the first suicide attacks in the country. In August 2003, a truck bomb exploded at the United Nations headquarters in Baghdad, killing the head of the UN delegation and several of its members. A few days later, Yassin Jarrad, the father of al Zarqawi's second wife, crashed a car laden with explosives into the Imam Ali mosque. The explosion killed 125 Shiites, among them Ayatollah Mohammed Baqer al Hakim, the spiritual leader of the Supreme Council of the Islamic Revolution in Iraq (SCIRI). The Ayatollah had only recently returned from Iran after the fall of Saddam Hussein, and was preparing to lead SCIRI to political victory in a democratic Iraq.[16]

At the time of the attacks, the connection between the two events escaped the scrutiny of Western analysts. In August 2003, it was a commonly held belief in the West that the conflict in Iraq was a bilateral struggle between Coalition forces and their supporters on one side, and Moqtada al Sadr's Shiite militia and Saddam's loyalists on the other. To the international jihadist movement, however, the message was well understood and assimilated. Al Zarqawi had signaled that the Iraqi conflict had two fronts, one against Coalition forces and the other against Shiites. And its main terror tactic was suicide missions.

From the end of August 2003 until December 2004, when Osama bin Laden officially recognized him as the head of al Qaeda in Iraq, the Jordanian led a group of jihadists known as Tawhid al Jihad, later renamed the Islamic State in Iraq (ISI). Bin Laden, however, disapproved of the ISI strategy of driving a wedge between the Sunni and Shia insurgencies, as he did not share their fear that a united nationalist resistance could emerge as a successful secular front in Iraq, marginalizing the jihadists. In the spring of 2004, al Zarqawi's fear was confirmed when Moqtada al Sadr's Shia revolt attracted the admiration of Sunni insurgents, who plastered pictures of the imam on the walls of Sunni neighborhoods. Bin Laden, it seemed, had been wrong. It was at this point that the Saudi decided to enfold al Zarqawi's group into al Qaeda, christening it al Qaeda in Iraq, and to join its sectarian war.

As emir of al Qaeda in Iraq, al Zarqawi was able to attract enough followers and resources to engage US forces, while keeping up the relentless succession of suicide bombings against Shiites that was carrying Iraq to the brink of civil war. His death in a US airstrike in 2006 prevented the outbreak of a sectarian war in Iraq, and temporarily crippled his organization.

From 2006 onward, a power struggle to gain control of al Qaeda in Iraq emerged. At the same time,[17] in an event known as the Sunni Awakening, elders convinced the population to turn their backs on the jihadists, regarding them as foreigners and enemies.[18] This, coupled with the American "surge" military strategy, resulted in the weakening of all jihadist groups in Iraq. Not until 2010, when Abu Bakr al Baghdadi became the leader of what was left of al Qaeda in Iraq, did things start to change.

Led by al Baghdadi, the group reverted to the original name of the Islamist State in Iraq and though it continued to attack US targets in Iraq, it began distancing itself from al Qaeda. Al Baghdadi was aware of the unpopularity of al Qaeda's brand among Sunni Iraqis following the Awakening, and purposely projected a more domestic and nationalistic image. He also realized that for the Sunni population, the Shiite government led by Prime Minister Maliki—which had openly discriminated against them using political tactics as well as violence—was even more unpopular than al Qaeda.[19] Accordingly, he attacked Shia targets, stoking the sectarian conflict.

It soon became apparent, however, that this strategy would not bear the desired fruit. The ISI was too small and too weak to make a difference. So al Baghdadi looked to the Syrian conflict as an opportunity to regroup and strengthen his organization.

In 2011, al Baghdadi dispatched a small number of jihadists to Syria. Traveling along the old smuggling routes across the deserts of northwestern Iraq, they acted as the vanguard of ISI, tasked with investigating whether the Syrian conflict provided concrete opportunities to grow militarily. Indeed, it did. The war-by-proxy fought in Syria not only equipped ISI members with military training, it also offered the financial means to relaunch the group, not as one of many jihadist armed organizations, but as a key player with its own territorial stronghold and military machine.

Unlike the leaders of al Qaeda, who eschewed territorial conquest to focus on the far-away enemy, i.e., the United States, al Baghdadi shared al Zarqawi's belief that without a large and strong territorial base in the Middle East their fight was destined to fail. His dream was as ambitious as the one that al Zarqawi had pursued: to recreate the Caliphate of Baghdad through a war of conquest against the near enemies—the corrupted, oligarchic elites who ruled Syria and Iraq, the Shiites.

In these countries, al Baghdadi followed a strategy al Zarqawi had set out years earlier, waging a traditional war of conquest door to door, occupying towns and cities and imposing Sharia rule on all of them. In Iraq, he went so far as to use military tactics developed by his predecessor, such as the Baghdad Belt, a strategy that would prove decisive to the construction of the Caliphate.[20]

The Baghdad Belt

The Baghdad Belt was al Zarqawi's code name for his plan to conquer Baghdad. Instead of seizing the city center, he planned to cut off the capital by progressively taking over towns in the surrounding "belt" region.

Originally, al Zarqawi planned to use ISI bases in the belts "to control access to Baghdad and funnel money, weapons, car bombs, and fighters into the city."[21] He also planned "to strangle the US helicopter air lanes by emplacing anti-aircraft cells along known routes in the belt areas around Baghdad."[22] The Belt itself was divided into five discrete regions: one in the south, comprising northern Babil and southern Diyala provinces; one in the west, comprising eastern Anbar province and the Thar Thar area; one in the north, comprising southern Salahaddin province and cities such as Taji; one in the east, comprising rural areas east of Baghdad; and the "Diyala Belt," which included Baqubah and Khalis.[23]

At the beginning of 2006, al Zarqawi's jihadists began

implementing the plan, initially taking Fallujah and most of Anbar province. In March and April they advanced toward Baghdad capturing Karma and Abu Ghraib. Finally they launched bombing attacks in northern Babil province and southern Baghdad. With much of the Belt under their control, the group consolidated its power in the Sunni stronghold. But in 2007 the Surge sent more than 130,000 US troops streaming into Iraq with the mission of reconquering the towns surrounding Baghdad, and the so called "triangle of death" south of the capital. Partnering with formations from the Sunni Awakening and Iraqi security forces numbering in the hundreds of thousands, the US operations lasted more than a year and "targeted the Islamic State in Iraq's (at the time part of al Qaeda in Iraq) command and control, training camps, and bases, as well as its Improvised Explosive Devices and suicide bomb factories." [24] At its close, the Surge was declared a success.

In the summer of 2014, al Baghdadi restored IS's formidable army to where ISI had been in 2007, at the end of the Baghdad Belt operation. In so doing, and moving further toward the establishment of the Caliphate, he achieved what al Zarqawi himself never had: the incorporation of the Baghdad Belt into a new state. It is no surprise, then, that many Sunnis in Iraq view al Baghdadi and the Islamic State as an Islamist phoenix, risen from the ashes of Abu Musab al Zarqawi's jihad.

Al Baghdadi the Modern Prophet

Though it was not until 2010, four years after al Zarqawi's death, that al Baghdadi stepped into his position of leader of al Qaeda in Iraq, the two men were part of the same operation for several years. With the start of the US invasion in 2003, al Baghdadi joined al Zarqawi's group, Tawhid al Jihad, with the task of smuggling foreign fighters into Iraq. Later he became the emir of Rawa, a town near the Syrian border, where he presided over his own Sharia court and "gained a reputation for brutality, publicly executing those suspected of aiding the US-led coalition forces."[25] In his governance of Rawa, one sees the seeds of al Baghdadi's administration of the Caliphate.

Like al Zarqawi, al Baghdadi focused on the day-to-day operations of the organization and avoided disseminating videos and making political pronouncements, common behavior among jihadist leaders. Only two known photos of al Baghdadi exist from before he was named Caliph. One shows a serious man with an olive complexion and round countenance. The other, released by the Iraqi government in January 2014, depicts an unsmiling, bearded figure in a black suit.[26] The image is cracked and blurry, as though it is a photo of a photo. During this period al Baghdadi covered his face even in front of his most trusted lieutenants, earning him the nickname "the invisible sheikh." The secrecy and mystery that surround the modern Caliph even now appear as the antithesis of parading and pontificating Western politicians and Arab dictators, whose ubiquitous images, plastered everywhere, boost their cults of personality.

Al Baghdadi's preference for avoiding the limelight may have been cultivated while serving a five-year prison sentence in Bucca Camp in southern Iraq after being captured by US forces in 2005. Like his Jordanian predecessor, he kept a very low profile in prison, misleading the Americans as to his true potential for leadership.[27]

Al Baghdadi possesses a background quite different from his predecessor's humble origins. Born in 1971 in Samarra, Iraq, al Baghdadi claims to be a direct descendant of the Prophet Mohammed. According to a widely cited biography released by jihadists, "he is a man from a religious family. His brothers and uncles include imams and professors of Arabic language, rhetoric and logic."[28] Al Baghdadi himself holds a degree in Islamic Studies from the University of Baghdad, and worked as an imam in the capital and in Fallujah prior to his capture. His academic training lends credibility to his interpretation of Islam and has furthered his image as a modern version of the Prophet. Not since Sheikh Azzam, the founder of the Muktab al Kidmat, the Arab-Afghan bureau, in Afghanistan, has a modern jihadist possessed such formal theological training. In his first official appearance after being elected Caliph, he spoke inside the Grand Mosque of Mosul, dressed in the traditional attire of an imam. His words were not those of a barbarous terrorist, but of a wise and pragmatic religious leader: "I am the wali [leader] who presides over you, though I am not the best of you, so if you see that I am right, assist me. If you see that I am wrong, advise me and put me on the right track, and obey me as long as I obey God in you."[29]

The Islamic State of Iraq and the Levant

As Caliph, al Baghdadi consolidated a few strongholds in Syria and attracted fighters from abroad using a skillful propaganda campaign. According to Shiraz Maher,[30] senior fellow at the International Centre for the Study of Radicalization at Kings College in London, al Baghdadi welcomed all newcomers, while other organizations, such as Jabhat al Nusra, regarded by many as a sort of franchise of al Qaeda in Syria, turned away potential recruits, fearing infiltrators. The ease of joining the ISI, coupled with its sophisticated media profile, boosted its popularity abroad, especially among young Muslims from the West.

In 2013 the ISI orchestrated a tactical merger with members of Jabhat al Nusra. This alliance gave birth to a new organization: the Islamic State of Iraq and the Levant (al Sham). It provoked the secession of several al Nusra's commanders—who rejected the merger—and triggered bitter infighting within the Sunni insurgency in Syria.

Despite the ideological similarities between al Jabhat Nusra and the ISI, many observers looked askance at the merger. While the former group had been engaged in overthrowing the Assad regime, the ISI had always been focused on its own territorial conquest. "ISIS did not conquer anything from Assad's forces, it engaged in battles with the rebels and other jihadist groups. Its strategy was to attack their position to carve its own enclave," says Francesca Borri, freelance journalist and author of *La Guerra Dentro*. Indeed, al Baghdadi never hid his plan to build an Islamic state inside war-torn Syria, and hence, the ISI appeared to many Syrians as a foreign occupier, while al Nusra had less ambitious plans.

Indeed, to the extent he did not refrain from attacks against sectarians as well as rival Sunni groups, al Baghdadi is regarded by many jihadists as a rogue commander. "The Islamic Front as well as the Free Syrian Army and other rebels consider ISIS as one of their enemies," explains Michael Przedlacki, the documentarian behind *Aleppo: Notes from the Dark*.[31] "Rogue commander" is a description that al Qaeda used to depict al Zarqawi after he masterminded the first suicide missions against Shiite targets in 2003. Ten years later, al Baghdadi's merger with al Nusra likewise enraged al Qaeda's leadership. Intervening in the matter, Ayman al Zawahiri rejected the merger and ordered al Baghdadi to return to Iraq, declaring the commanders of al Nusra the true representatives of al Qaeda in Syria.

Just as in 2003 al Zarqawi ignored al Qaeda's criticism, in 2013 al Baghdadi's response to al Zawahiri's orders was defiant: "I have to choose between the rule of

God and the rule of al Zawahiri, and I choose the rule of God."[32] These simple words confirmed the growing weakness of al Qaeda, as compared with the rising star of the Islamic State's leadership. "For the last 10 years or more, [al Zawahiri] has been holed up in the Afghanistan-Pakistan border area and hasn't really done very much more than issue a few statements and videos," Richard Barrett, a former counter-terrorism chief with the British foreign intelligence service, told Agence France-Presse. "Whereas al Baghdadi has done an amazing amount—he has captured cities, he has mobilized huge amounts of people, he is killing ruthlessly throughout Iraq and Syria. . . . If you were a guy who wanted action, you would go with al Baghdadi."[33]

It is undeniable that the popularity of the Islamic State springs from the appeal of its extraordinary military successes to a population defeated after decades of ruthless ruling by Western-backed Arab leaders, people disillusioned by the corruption inside the PLO and Hamas, and depressed by a seemingly unending period of sectarian infighting, war, and sanctions.

Against the background of a civil war in Syria, and an Iraq still hobbled by Western intervention, IS has eschewed fatwas and religious lectures, instead gaining followers with promises of political deliverance in the restoration of the Caliphate. The acceptance of this new state, however, comes at a considerable price to followers in search of a lasting political solution to decades of war and destruction. It requires subjects to accept its strict rules, rough justice, and the second-class citizenship of women. Furthermore, as IS's sectarian offensives show, neither Shiites nor followers of any other faith have any place in this future state, unless they embrace Salafism.

For all their brutality, however, the Islamic State and al Baghdadi seem to have put forward a program that resonates with persecuted Sunnis. For now, this new entity is only a shell-state, a body that possesses the socio-economic infrastructure of a state, but lacks the political recognition and popular consensus of a true state. Even as, in the fall of 2014, the US announces a three-year program of air strikes to thwart the group, al Baghdadi is working to change that. The Islamic State's goal seems closer than ever.

Chapter Two

Rehearsals for the Caliphate

The Caliphate does not represent the sole historical attempt of an armed organization to construct its own shell-state. Decades ago, the PLO successfully formed a shell-state after gaining independence from its sponsors and effectively privatizing the business of terrorism. Ironically, the achievement came as a surprise to the Israelis, just as the West was shocked when in the summer of 2014 it discovered IS's independent wealth. Against the absurd claims of counter-terrorism experts that they could not have foreseen the rise of the Islamic State in the firmament of jihadist groups—if not through its military conquests, then via its successful financial endeavors—the history of the PLO's financial independence bears recalling.

In December 1987, the Palestinians living in the Gaza Strip and the West Bank launched the Intifada. This spontaneous uprising triggered a distinct shift in Israeli policy. The government no longer tolerated "unofficial" inflows of money into the Occupied Territories and ordered the police to block the smuggling of money across all transit points.

In the following year, over $20 million in cash was confiscated. Yet this did little to curb the PLO's economic support in the Occupied Territories. Money earned through legitimate, often sophisticated, routes was plentiful.[34]

What the Israelis soon discovered was that Arafat had transformed a loose confederation of armed groups, financed by various sponsors, into a complex self-funded economic organization. It acted as a *de facto* state in the territories it controlled, thanks to various legitimate and illegitimate activities, ranging from export of textiles to drug smuggling.[35] The PLO generated annual revenue in excess of the gross national product of a number of Arab countries.

With these revenues, Arafat effectively ran Gaza and the West Bank free of the control of his former sponsors. However, with money but without political recognition, the Occupied Territories could not be defined as a proper state, but only as shell-state, a state that possesses national infrastructure but lacks the self-determination that is the core of nationhood. In the standard nation-building model, the economy and the infrastructure of the modern state are built after the process of self-determination has produced political integration. In the shell-state model established by the PLO, and now adopted by the Islamic State, economy and infrastructure building precede political recognition. Self-determination then, remains an elusive, contingent fact. But not, as we shall see, in the intentions of IS.

The Modern Version of the War-by-Proxy

During the Cold War, shell-states often emerged out of proxy wars. That is, states sponsored non-state actors to wage their wars-by-proxy, and some of these armed organizations followed the lead of the PLO to achieve economic independence and built state infrastructures of their own. Since 2011, a similar transformation has been at work inside the war-torn regions of Syria and Iraq. Just as during the Cold War Arafat used donations from Arab sponsors as seed capital to build the independent wealth of the PLO in the Occupied Territories, so too Abu Bakr al Baghdadi financially exploited Arab state sponsors seeking a regime change in Syria to carve out his group's economic stronghold. What differs today is the wide range of state sponsors available to proxy groups and the misalignment of sponsors' interests.

In Syria, it has been relatively easy for any jihadist group to choose among an array of financial backers—in a sense, to shop around for sponsors. During the Cold War, instead, proxies had only two choices, i.e., one of the two superpowers. The advent of a multipolar world crowded the field of sponsors and in the process transformed the war-by-proxy into a sort of betting ground. When in 2010 al Baghdadi went in search of sponsors, the Kuwaitis, Qataris, and Saudis lined up, in the process indirectly providing IS access to Western military equipment—a luxury that Arafat never enjoyed.[36]

What has not changed is the increased difficulty proxies pose to finding peaceful solutions to conflicts. This is particularly true of the modern proxy war, in particular, due to the absurd and paradoxical conflicts of interest among sponsors. In Syria, Iran has backed the regime of Bashar al-Assad, mostly through its Lebanese branch, Hezbollah, while the Saudis, the Kuwaitis, and the Qataris have bankrolled a plethora of Sunni insurgent groups, including the former ISIS, to undermine Iranian power in the region. Hezbollah in turn has been arming and funding Hamas in the Palestinian conflict, though Hamas is predominantly Sunni, and historically has been bankrolled by Saudi Arabia.[37] In the summer of 2014, Hamas used both Iranian drones (claiming they were built in Gaza) and Syrian-made long-range missiles (likely supplied by the Islamic State) to attack Israel.

To complicate the picture, Russia is arming the Assad regime in Syria while Washington arms the anti-Assad Syrian rebels with, ironically, weapons that IS confiscates after each victory. In April 2014, *Time* magazine reported, "Syrian fighters are now using U.S.-made anti-tank weapons against Assad's forces. Experts say it is unlikely those weapons could have wound up in Syria without US approval."[38] Then, on September 10, 2014, President Obama announced in a nationwide address that the US would bomb the Islamic State in Syria, to which Damascus, backed by Moscow, replied that without its approval and permission such action would be an aggression. In the modern war-by-proxy, alliances are never clear and can change overnight.

The diplomatic terrain in which all these parties move is also shifting constantly, at times to absurd effect. In August 2014, militants from the Kurdistan Workers' Party (PKK) came to the aid of the Peshmerga against the Islamic State, which was advancing in the autonomous region in Northern Iraq. The US, meanwhile, provided air strikes to aid the Peshmerga. The curious result was *de facto* cooperation between the PKK and the US, though the PKK remains on the US's official terrorist list. The Europeans also agreed to arm the Kurdish army, and so technically are also fighting with the PKK. And because Turkey is part of the grand coalition organized by Obama to defeat the Islamic State, the PKK and Ankara, historical enemies, are on the same side.[39]

At the end of the summer of 2014, the United States organized the grand coalition under the NATO umbrella to fight IS. This might give the impression that the Islamic State is uniting old and new enemies, and that the time of irrational alliances had come to an end. This is not the case. In mid-September 2014, for example, Iran and Syria, the two largest Shia states in the Middle East, were not invited to participate in the Paris Conference, apparently because Saudi Arabia and Qatar had vetoed their presence. The coalition and the conference did not flesh out any new strategy to address the problems of the region, and the gathering turned out to be yet another opportunity for a group photo of world leaders.

Indeed, none of the NATO or Arab countries has officially agreed to send troops to fight the Islamic State. On the contrary, they will continue to participate in the conflict by proxy, while pursuing their own interests. Paradoxically, the grand coalition, instead of stopping this process, risks adding more rich countries to the long list of sponsors.

Even the Assad regime uses proxy groups to fight the rebels and the jihadists and to repress the local population. Hezbollah and Iranian fighters have been deployed in Syria instead of the corrupted Syrian army. "In March 2012 I lived in Southern Lebanon," recounts Francesca Borri. "Every week the bodies of Hezbollah's militants in Syria were carried back for their funerals."[40]

Against this background, al Baghdadi may cleverly continue taking advantage of the political paradoxes of the modern war-by-proxy. Thus far, showing a remarkable understanding of his sponsors' wishes and perspectives, he has exploited the proliferation of small jihadist and rebel groups to enlarge his own organization, through either mergers or military victories against rival Sunni groups. "In Aleppo and Syria often fighters move from one faction to another," explains a former Syrian rebel who escaped via Turkey. "ISIS appealed to many because it was better organized, more efficient than the others. Its fighters seemed better trained. You must understand that most of the people who participate in this war have no idea how to fight—they are kids, from Syria and all over the world. The foreigners, in particular, are excited at the idea of going to war. But they don't even know how to shoot a gun. Among all these groups, the Islamic State projects the most professional image, so people believe they will be trained. At the same time, it appears determined to gain control of selected key targets. If you want to fight you may as well join the best."[41]

From 2011 to 2014, betting on an international nonintervention in Syria, al Baghdadi has carved out his main territorial stronghold in Syria, ironically using the money of the Arab sponsors and attacking and conquering rival rebels' positions. Foreseeing a long-term conflict in Syria, he sought to gain control of vast sections of the market for arms in that country.

Clearly, the Islamic State's successful exploitation of the modern war-by-proxy in the Middle East springs from the contradictions of this type of conflict in a multipolar, post–Cold War environment. This is unlikely to be changed by the formation of a grand coalition, as proven by the exclusion of Iran, major sponsor of the regime of Assad, and the lack of united strategy. Indeed, such contradictions explain the difficulties that, since 2011, the United States has encountered in rallying any type of alliance of forces in the region to address the regime change in Damascus and, more recently, the threat posed by the Caliphate. As we shall see in the last chapter, the grand coalition has not resolved the foreign policy contradictions that prevent any fruitful resolution of the problems of the Middle East.

What the West is ignoring, either because of ignorance or because of convenience, is the anarchy into which Northern Syria has been plunged by a war-by-proxy bankrolled though a plethora of sponsors. "Society has broken down. Those who could flee have left and those who have remained are too poor or to old to leave," explains Francesca Borri, for a long time the sole Western journalist in Aleppo. "What we have in Northern Syria is no longer what we had before the beginning of civil war but something different, not at all representative of what the Syrian population was. Those who prey upon the population are criminal groups, responsible also for most of the kidnappings of Westerners, mostly journalists and aid workers."[42] This is a scenario similar to the one we find in regions of the world where the authority of the state, often an authoritarian one, has broken down, creating a political vacuum that sectarian armed organizations fill with violence. In this anarchic environment, society has ceased to exist, replaced by perennial, pre-modern warfare. "Inside and outside Aleppo, warlords are the supreme authority, and this is true also for the Islamic State," explains Borri. "The ultimate loyalty of the fighters is to their commander, not the leadership of the organization." However, unlike the other groups, the Caliphate provides a hierarchic military and administrative structure that, though rudimentary, reduces the danger that its battalions will degenerate into militias or criminal groups.

As in Nigeria or Sahel or Afghanistan, hostages are

precious merchandise, and, as in Lebanon in the 1990s, these goods are resold several times over in a market rife with criminal and terror groups. The facility with which journalists are kidnapped confirms the sectarian, pre-modern nature of the conflict in Syria. "Most of the colleagues who have been kidnapped were traveling with drivers and bodyguards provided by one of the many rebel groups, and were kidnapped at roadblocks by rival rebel groups traveling in a highly fragmented zone," explains Borri. "I was lucky because I used al Qaeda's protection and traveled inside an area at the time controlled by ISIS. I also use a disguise. I pretended to be a Syrian refugee. I didn't carry even a pen, and was covered up head to toe."

Often the sponsors involved in this despicable trade use ransom payments to hide their sponsorship. This seems to be the case with the $20 million ransom that Qatar paid al Nusra to free forty-five UN soldiers from the Fiji islands who had been kidnapped in the Golan Heights.[43]

World public opinion is equally disinclined to approve any intervention similar to that carried out in Libya. The fiasco of Bush and Blair's war in Iraq has proven that military intervention is not the best solution to bring peace to the Middle East. On the contrary, it may produce Frankensteins like the Islamic State.

The Islamic State shows a remarkable understanding of the frustration of Western public opinion when confronted with the situation in the Middle East. The videos of kidnapped British journalist John Cantlie[44] aim at denouncing the double standards of Western govern-ments in dealing with kidnapping. While every other government negotiates and pays, the US and British refuse to do so. Al Baghdadi and his followers seems to be well aware of the idiosyncrasies of the current world order, very different from those of the Cold War, and their way of reaping revenge on a militarily superior enemy is to expose them to world public opinion. They also know that the proxy war fought in Syria and Iraq will only boo-merang against its sponsors, weakening these states in the process. At present, Western and Arab powers seem unaware of all of these developments.

Privatizing Terrorism

The best proof that the war-by-proxy is an obsolete instru-ment of nation-building is found in the successes of the Islamic State. Unlike other sponsored groups engaged in overthrowing the Assad regime in Damascus, al Bagh-dadi's warriors have been able to carve out a territorial stronghold in Syria and now also in Iraq. As a former US Marine recounted in the *New Yorker*: "My visit coincided with the day ISIS seized the city of Azaz from the Free Syrian Army's Northern Storm Brigade [. . .] Seeing this, it seemed irrefutable that ISIS, although characterized as a rebel group in the Syrian civil war, did not consider the toppling of the Assad régime to be its primary objective. If it had, it wouldn't have wasted resources seizing Azaz, a city held by the rebels since March 2012. ISIS's war wasn't part of the revolution. It was a conquest all its own."[45]

The key to IS's success has been the speed with which it has privatized terrorism in comparison to other groups such as the PLO or the IRA. IS gained financial independence from its sponsors with remarkable celerity, as it was virtually unopposed when it made the economic transition. The truth is, IS's sponsors have been powerless, as they can find no proxy strong enough to challenge the organization. The proliferation of sponsored groups has backfired, producing a plethora of small and weak armed organizations. Among such a fragmented jihadist and rebel front, it was easy for the Islamic State of Iraq and Syria to fight its own war of conquest and seize, in less than a couple of years, strategic regions rich in resources, such as the oil fields of eastern Syria, often in the hands of smaller rebel groups, militias, and war-lords.

Further contributing to IS's independence were al Baghdadi's clever alliances with local Sunni tribes to exploit such resources. Working together, they arranged for the extraction and smuggling of oil, some of which was even sold back to the Syrian government. By so doing, al Baghdadi forestalled any opposition on the part of the local population, and projected the image of a more honest and equitable power than the Assad regime. Politically, the ability to cooperate with local leaders, to co-opt them into the Caliphate as partners, not as a conquered population but as citizens of a modern state, has allowed the Islamic State to grow exponentially among militants as well as to strengthen its political claim to recreate the Caliphate. Against this background, it would be a mistake to regard IS's territorial strongholds only as military bases. They represent the necessary pillars of a modern Islamist state that seeks legitimacy through consensus at the local level in the very regions it has occupied through a war of conquest.

Though traditionally shell-states run by armed groups have shunned the participation of local authorities, the Islamic State pioneered this strategy even before al Baghdadi was elected Caliph. While advancing toward Baghdad in the summer of 2014, IS launched an attack on the Baiji oil refinery, the largest in the country. At the same time, it targeted the Haditha Dam on the Euphrates River in northwestern Iraq, as well as sections of the 600,000-barrel-a-day pipeline to Turkey, which, as of this writing, has not operated since March 2014. As in Syria, the management of these resources was shared in Iraq with the local Sunni communities, tribes that had been discriminated against by the governing regime. This tactic not only prevented their opposition, but also gained their support and consensus.

In all his dealings with Iraqi Sunni tribes, al Baghdadi has applied remarkably modern diplomatic tactics to win their support. In Anbar, he avoided stirring up bad memories of al Qaeda's attacks on the participants in the Sunni Awakening. "Al Baghdadi's fighters have not harmed religious men, the Anbar tribes, including those who formed the Sahwa forces, or even the police force. When the tribes refused to raise ISIS banners in Fallujah, he ordered his fighters not to raise the banner or try to co-opt the fighters of armed groups, clans or religious men. . . . However, the banner did appear on certain occasions, such as when ISIS kidnapped and killed a number of Iraqi soldiers in the area of Albu Bali in north Fallujah in mid-January of this year. Al Baghdadi's appeasement policies in Anbar have once again revealed a pragmatism that was lacking in al-Qaeda's previous leaders."[46]

Al Baghdadi's willingness to foster these alliances with local Sunni tribes is part of his strategy to speed up the process of independence from his sponsors. Financial independence, however, is not born exclusively from a desire to break with foreign sponsors. Rather, the privatization of terrorism offers IS tools to enforce loyalty among its fighters. That is, al Baghdadi has sought financial independence as an inoculation against the corruption of his forces. Corruption has been the downfall of many armed organizations and of all Arab regimes, without exception. Sponsorship, accordingly, is well known to breed a culture of bribery.

One such lesson from history is Arafat's downfall, a result of the PLO's swelling coffers. By the time the PLO was managing an annual budget of $8 to $12 billion, its structure and leadership had been fully compromised. Bribes and corruption generated by a political culture of sponsorship represented a blight of which the group was never fully cured.[47]

Carving Out the First Islamist Shell-State in Syria

While privatizing terrorism, the Islamic State discovered that the shell-state model was a perfect vehicle to achieve the ambitious nation-building goal of recreating the Caliphate. A shell-state can be as small as a suburb or as large as a proper state. A shell-state is simple to construct and manage, because political integration is often absent. Its ideal ground is found in war-torn enclaves where all infrastructure has collapsed and political authority has disappeared. Rulers monopolize political power and need to seek democratic consensus. In assembling the shell-state, therefore, economics trumps politics. And a shell-state has the further benefit of being inexpensive to run, because its economic sphere is limited to the war economy and the privatization of terror. Non-military expenses are minimal and the population need only be provided with bare sustenance.

In the traditional shell-state model, war is the sole source of income. "War is our way of life," declared a Northern Alliance fighter from the Shomali Plain in Afghanistan. Accordingly, fighters are highly paid in comparison with the rest of the population.[48] In sharp contrast, the economy of the Caliphate does not exclusively depend upon the economy of the war of conquest, nor are its jihadists semi-mercenaries motivated by high salaries. Indeed, despite its need to assure their loyalty, the Islamic State pays its fighters less than what a blue-collar civilian earns in Syria or Iraq. Declassified documents show that, over a period for which the Department of Defense kept records, "the average Islamic State foot soldier earned a base salary of just $41 a month, far lower than blue-collar Iraq jobs such as a bricklayer making $150 a month. As counter-terrorism experts have long suspected, the members of a group like the Islamic State are so ideologically driven that economic incentives to stop the flow of fighters aren't likely to have much impact."[49]

If the Islamic State's army is not primarily motivated by money, it is driven by a higher cause: the achievement of the modern Caliphate, an ideal Muslim state that transcends all, including personal wealth. Such political construction should be regarded as a sign of modernity in the Middle East, a region where nation-building has been for centuries the sport of foreign powers seeking their own interest with the help of corrupted local elites.

Although al Baghdadi's war of conquest in the Middle East is reminiscent of pre-modern conflicts, the discipline and ideals of the Caliphate represent a step toward a proper state different from the shell-state of the Taliban in Afghanistan or the FARC in Colombia, whose aims are primarily to prey, financially and otherwise, upon the local population. The Islamic State's warriors also represent a step forward vis-à-vis the jihadists of al Zarqawi, all potential suicide bombers, eager to become martyrs and spend eternity with seventy-two virgins. Though al Baghdadi's men are willing to die for the Caliphate, their dream, by contrast, is positive and contemporary: they want to experience the Caliphate on this earth, not only in the afterlife. Like Israel for Zionist Jews, the recreation of a strong Islamic state in the land of the forefathers represents deliverance in this life to some Muslims. This is a powerful, positive message for a population that is ready to hear it.

Seeking Consensus Inside the Shell-State

Rather paradoxically, the support of the population inside the state-shell is as important to al Baghdadi as is the commitment of his warriors. As proven by the Iranian Revolution, divine right alone is not enough to secure the functioning of the state. Nor can the Caliphate become a gigantic prison, as Taliban-controlled Afghanistan was. Unlike the Taliban, who behaved as a superior caste and preyed upon the local Afghan population, al Baghdadi aims to found a modern state, complete with the consent of the governed, even if the definition of the citizenry itself is limited by sectarianism and does not include the active participation of women. Key to this consent is the provision of social programs.

As has been reported in the *Atlantic*, in Syria and Iraq "IS helps run bread factories and provides fruits and vegetables to many families, passing the goods out personally. In Raqqa, ISIS has established a food kitchen to feed the needy and an Office for Orphans to help pair them with families. IS militants have developed health and welfare programs in the enclaves under their control, using the organization's own funds. The Taliban may be paranoid and skeptical about vaccination campaigns, but IS conducts polio vaccination campaigns to arrest the spread of the disease." Social programs,[50] then, are the other side of the coin of the Islamic State's barbarous sectarian dictatorship.[51]

It is important to point out that those who carry out social work are different from the fighters. "The distinction between civilians and fighter militants is fundamental. They are two different things," explains Michael Przedlacki.[52] If it is deemed necessary, fighters will prey upon the local population while civilian militants protect it. Inside the Caliphate, the distinction between these two types of militants is arranged to maximize the efficiency of the shell-state.

Moreover, the provision of social programs represents the fruit of IS's economic strategy. That is hardly by mistake. Even before IS fighters had literally bulldozed sections of the border between Iraq and Syria to announce the birth of the Caliphate, revenues were plentiful. For example, for over a year the group has been running a profitable smuggling business along the Turkish and Syrian borders,[53] even taking a cut of the humanitarian aid coming into Syria. Thanks to the clever plan of action carried out during its three-year privatization of terrorism, today the Islamic State does not need to prey upon the local population like other groups. As the *Atlantic* reported, when IS seized $425 million from Mosul's central bank, the monies were earmarked to underwrite not only military aid but also "the group's campaign to win hearts and minds."[54] Such events demonstrate an integration of the finances of the armed group, the Islamic State, and of its shell-state, the Caliphate.

The merging of IS funds with the shell-state's finances and business partnerships with local tribes also proves the organization's commitment to nation-building and demonstrates its application of some of the basic administrative principles of the modern nation state. Finally, the rechanneling of wealth inside the shell-state not only makes the Caliphate stronger militarily, but also solidifies consensus among the population.

The governorate of al Raqqa in Syria, where the headquarters of the Caliphate is located, offers several examples of public works bankrolled through the profits generated by the privatization of terrorism, such as the completion of a new *souk*, or public market, welcomed by the local population. The Islamic State also "runs an electricity office that monitors electricity-use levels, installs power lines, and hosts workshops on how to repair old ones. The militants fix potholes, bus residents between the territories they control, rehabilitate blighted medians to make roads more aesthetically pleasing, and operate a post office and *zakat* (almsgiving) office, which the group claims has helped farmers with their harvests. Most importantly for Syrians and Iraqis downriver, IS has continued operating the Tishrin Dam (renaming it al Faruq) on the Euphrates River. Through all of these offices and departments, IS is able to offer a semblance of stability in unstable and marginalized areas, even if many locals do not like its ideological program."[55] The pursuit of this type of stability through the rule of an armed organization is not atypical in regions that have suffered protracted conflicts. For example, in 1998, the Colombian government demilitarized an area the size of Switzerland encompassing the municipalities of San Vicente del Caguan, La Macarena, Vista Hermosa, Mesetas, and Uribe. The area, which became known as Despeje, was given to FARC, the Marxist armed organization, as a gesture of goodwill in bringing the country's civil war to a peaceful conclusion. In this region FARC carried out social and public works. It built and paved new roads and improved the town's communal areas, utilizing forced labor. It provided people with security, a luxury they had long lacked.[56] However, none of the shell-states constructed by armed organizations has successfully completed the transition into a real state.

As we shall see in the following chapter, the Islamic State believes that this goal could be achieved by including local authorities and populations in the political construction of the Caliphate.

Chapter Three

The Paradox of the New Rome

In June 2014, two days before the beginning of the holy month of Ramadan, ISIS released a statement announcing the establishment of the Caliphate targeted at Muslim audiences around the world. "Shake off the dust of humiliation and disgrace," said its spokesman, and, in the words of journalist Jeremy Bowen, "a new caliphate will rise out of the chaos, confusion and despair of the modern Middle East."[57]

The following day, the Islamic State uploaded a sleek video of a bearded fighter from Chile named Abu Safiyya presenting a newly demolished border post between Syria and Iraq. Titled "The End of Sykes-Picot,"[58] the video announced the forthcoming obliteration at the hands of the Islamic State of two political entities created by the British and the French in 1916, i.e., Syria and Iraq. Starring a Chilean Muslim, the video projected to the Umma, the global community of Muslims, an image of the Islamic State as both cosmopolitan and real, with a global reach.

With the help of modern technology and through social media channels, therefore, the Islamic State attempts to present a contemporary political image of itself, a positive image in sharp contrast with decadent and malfunctioning Western democracies or "Western-inspired" Muslim regimes. "Look at Egypt. Look at the way it ended for Muslims who cast their vote for [deposed President] Mohammed Morsi and believed in your democracy, in your lies. Democracy doesn't exist. Do you think you are free?" boasted a member of the Islamic State. "The West is ruled by banks, not by parliaments, and you know that. You know that you're just a pawn, except you have no courage. You think of yourself, your job, your house . . . because you know you have no power. But fortunately, the jihad has started. Islam will get to you and bring you freedom."[59]

In presenting a new Caliphate, the Islamic State attempts to offer a contemporary political image of itself analogous to that which the early Zionists projected, though the word democracy is not so valued by IS as it was by Israel's founders. In the 1940s, Jews from different parts of the world joined in a struggle against the British to reconquer their ancient land, a "God-given" ancestral home where they could seek deliverance once again. Just as ancient Israel for the Jews has always been the Promised Land, the Caliphate represents for Muslims the ideal state, the perfect nation, wherein to receive deliverance after centuries of humiliation, racism, and defeat at the hands of the infidels, i.e., foreign powers, and their Muslim partners. As modern Jews built a contemporary version of ancient Israel for all the Jews of the world, the Islamic State is engaged in constructing a functional Islamic country for all Sunnis in the twenty-first century. At least this is what its propaganda tells us.

Although it may seem absurd and repulsive to compare the barbarous behavior of members of the Islamic State with the conduct of the founding fathers of Israel, this is how the struggle to build the Caliphate is perceived among its followers and sympathizers. And this message is particularly powerful today amid the wreckage of Middle Eastern politics. Indeed, the war in Iraq and Syria is acting as a catalyst, magnifying the belief that the solution to all Middle Eastern political problems rests in the contemporary rebirth of the Caliphate.

Regardless of the violence that the Islamic State uses to reconstruct this entity, and in spite of it, the cosmopolitan and transcendent nature of the contemporary Caliphate is as powerful to Sunnis as their collective memory of the original Caliphate. For decades, Islamists and Islamic scholars have insisted that the greatness and splendor of the Caliphate, that heaven on earth, will be recreated. "The restoration of the Caliphate has been a dream of Islamic revivalists since at least the 1950s, when Hizb ut Tahrir began calling for its restoration. The Taliban leader Mullah Omar went as far as claiming for himself one of the caliph's traditional titles, Amir al Mu'minin, the 'Commander of the Believers.' The restoration of the Caliphate was often mentioned by Osama bin Laden as his ultimate goal."[60] But none of those men ever got close to its realization, and for them the Caliphate remained nothing more than a sweet, impossible dream.

Abu Bakr al Baghdadi is the first Islamic leader since the 31st Caliph, Abdülmecid II (1823–61), to claim this title, and to satisfy the nostalgia for a lost world, a society associated with the golden age of early Islam, when, under the leadership of the first four caliphs, successors of the Prophet, Islam expanded territorially and blossomed culturally.[61]

Against this background it is easy to understand why generations of Sunni radicals have dreamt of the moment when the twentieth-century Arabian borders drawn by European powers would be erased. And it is the Islamic State, not al Qaeda, that has brought this dream to fruition.

The Tool of Violence

The power of history, of past splendor, coupled with a destiny linked to a promised land, a territory chosen by God for His people, feeds a seductive nostalgia. We have seen it in the process of the formation of the state of Israel as well as in the revolution that Khomeini led in 1978 in the former Persia. On wings of violence, the Iranian Revolution brought the past into the present and projected it into a future hoped to be even more splendid.[62]

The repackaging of a timeless religious past into modern constitutions seems to be a recurrent feature of our present—take Israel and Iran, for example. Because the reclamation of past splendor takes place under the banner of violence—through revolutions, civil wars, terrorism, and wars of conquest—it is difficult to disassociate from the sheer brutality of the process until it has run its full course. This is true for the Zionist armed groups of the 1940s as well as for the Revolutionary Guards of Khomeini's revolution. In other words, all we see is the violent means to remake the present using the blueprint of the past, so that often we miss the true goal of such endeavor.

Although it is an integral part of the remodeling of the past, violence is only a means to an end. It is a tactic designed to terrorize, to instill fear in the enemy in order to offset the asymmetry of a war fought against well-equipped armies, like the Persian army in 1978, or the British army in Palestine in the 1940s.

Contrary to what the Western media has reported, the Caliphate is no more violent and barbarous than any armed organization in recent memory. In Kosovo in the 1990s, similar atrocities were committed, including cutting off children's heads to play football with them in front of their parents.[63] What distinguishes the Islamic State is the technological use of such barbarities to promote its cause, linking them to world news. On the eve of the 2014 World Cup, for example, IS documented on Twitter a football match in which its members played soccer with the severed heads of their opponents.[64]

Today, technology offers contemporary armed organizations the possibility of taking the propaganda of violence to new, higher levels. For example, while the Serbs could not widely disseminate evidence of their atrocities, the video of the beheading of James Foley went viral in a few hours. The message of fear was limited to a global, not a local audience. The absence of social media, and broadcasters' and advertisers' preference for bloodless and sanitized wars, shielded us from the horrendous actions and crimes perpetrated in Kosovo. Today, the Islamic State's atrocities reach us in real time on social media and are rebroadcast by a mainstream media constantly playing catch-up with Facebook, YouTube, and other sites. Even when censorship is attempted, as was the case in the video of Foley's beheading, social media easily bypasses it.

Technology does not change nor inflate the nature of the violent messages that armed organizations broadcast. The propaganda remains to spread fear among enemies and proselytize among potential followers. "How did I feel when I saw those guys play football with the heads of Shiite Iraqi soldiers and policemen? I felt that finally justice was done," a Sunni man I interviewed stated. About being driven from his home in Baghdad, he continued, "The Militia came to kick us out and the police were outside, laughing. We had to leave everything behind, our furniture, our clothes, the children's toys. We were allowed to take only what we could carry."[65] For this man, witnessing IS's unspeakable brutality to one Shiite was a form of reprisal against all Shia. Whether the acts are viewed on a screen or witnessed in the streets of Fallujah, as was the dragging of the bodies of the tortured Blackwater employees, the effect is the same.

Social media is not the only tool that IS uses to spread its message of fear and express the scope of its territorial power. The numbers also help tell the story. In *al Naba* ("The News"), the Islamic State's annual business report, in 2013 the organization "claimed nearly 10,000 operations in Iraq: 1,000 assassinations, 4,000 improvised explosive devices planted and hundreds of radical prisoners freed."[66] Considered in light of the fact that in 2013 an approximate total of 7,800 people were killed in Iraq, IS's claims are astounding.[67] In the same report the Islamic State claims that in 2014 hundreds of "apostates" had been turned, confirming the powerful proselytizing force of violence at the hands of a victorious army. In a bloody sectarian war, a dehumanized and defeated opponent may seek protection by joining the winner.

The rising number of followers around the world, people seduced and lured into violence by the propaganda of the Islamic State, confirms the global appeal of its message: a message that the virtual world in which we now live can also produce new, irrational, and barbaric acts of violence. The failed attempt by a group of Australian Muslims to randomly kidnap and behead an individual, simply to post its execution online, shows us the potential degeneration of the Islamic State propaganda narrative in a virtual environment where everything is a video game, including real-life warfare. This mutation of the effects of the classic propaganda by the errant atrocities of armed organizations poses a completely novel threat to Western countries. Like the improvised suicide bombers of the early 2000s, the do-it-yourself Islamist decapitators of today are difficult to track down because they do not belong to any established groups for long enough, their radicalization having taken place in the space of a few mouse clicks.

While the Islamic State is terrifying to a global audience, as distinguished from the Taliban and al Qaeda, it is also a protector of the local population, in whose defense no form of revenge or punishment is too ruthless. The surprisingly sophisticated bureaucracy of the Islamic State typically includes an Islamic court system and a roving police force, which carries out its sentences publicly, in the streets or public squares. "In the Syrian town of Manbij, for example, IS officials cut off the hands of four robbers . . . [,] whipped individuals for insulting their neighbors, confiscated and destroyed counterfeit medicine, and on multiple occasions summarily executed and crucified individuals for apostasy or murder."[68]

For Westerners these are not the acts of a modern state that seeks legitimacy through consensus, but of a brutal occupying military force, a sadistic army. However, this is not necessarily the view Syrian and Iraqi Sunnis take after decades of chaos, war, destruction, and corruption at the hands of civil servants, policemen, and politicians. "You look only at the executions," explains an IS member. "But every war has its executions, its traitors, its spies. We set up soup kitchens, we rebuilt schools, hospitals, we restored water and electricity, we paid for food and fuel. While the UN wasn't even able to deliver humanitarian aid, we were vaccinating children against polio. It's just that some actions are more visible than others. For every thief we punish, you punish a hundred children with your indifference."[69]

To understand the appeal that the political construction of the Islamic State holds to the local Sunni population, as well as the real challenge that the Caliphate poses to the world, one needs to step back in time and consider nation-building in the context of pre-modern tribal society.

Rome, the Modern Troy

Together with its pre-modern dictatorship and barbarity, the Islamic State promotes its bid for statehood with an ancient message of home and hearth. It encourages its soldiers to marry and, during victory marches, it parades its fighters flanked by machine gun–bearing children. In Raqqa, the capital of the Caliphate, a propaganda van actively recruits young residents to enroll in training camps where they will learn how to use modern weapons. On warm summer evenings, residents are invited to attend Islamic summer festivals in public squares. There is music, laughter, and praise for the Caliphate and Caliph. Kids flock to these events, drawn by the music and the fascinating display of arms and assembled fighters, who encourage them to join them in the defense of their new state.[70]

Although the world that the Caliphate depicts on social media is always seen against the background of a war of conquest that recalls the Middle Ages—with severed heads and the bodies of the crucified displayed in public parks or squares, and women not to be seen—another aspect of the Caliphate does exist. Indeed, its social face shows traces of humanity, and it is this side to which the West must respond if it wishes to slow recruitment.

Unlike the Taliban, the Islamic State seeks legitimacy among the civilian population by luring men, women, and children into its Caliphate as citizens. Unlike the PLO, ETA, and the IRA, which each felt legitimated by only a segment of the population, the Islamic State pursues the approval of the Umma, the worldwide community of all believers, the soul of Islam. Accordingly, its ambitions go well beyond those of previous armed groups. Having proven with spectacular military successes that God is on their side, and that the heir of the Prophet, the Caliph, has come back, the Islamic State's warriors must now win the support of the people of Allah and the love of his women to produce the next generation.

To find a similarly ambitious nation-building project springing from total violence, legitimized by supernatural power, and drenched in nostalgia for a lost golden age, one has to go back in time to pre-modern tribal societies and to the birth of ancient Rome.

Roman mythology traces a direct bloodline from the survivors of Troy to the founders of Rome. Romulus and Remus are presented as the descendants of the prince Aeneas, and his son, Ascanius, who miraculously escaped the destruction of Troy. Naturally, destiny plays a major role in the maintenance of this blood line, a sign that Troy could not die at the hands of men but was destined to relive its splendor through Rome. Yet Rome was not a mere replica, the new Troy. Rather, it was its modern incarnation. Likewise, in the words of its Caliph, the Islamic Caliphate will not be a mere replica. It will have its own identity in tune with modern times.

Against a mythological background that provided legitimacy to the newly founded city, Rome had to solve practical problems related to nation-building: to populate the enclave and transform it from a military campground of extremely violent men into a proper town. This transition required the formation of families. Hence the Romans sought women to populate their newly built city. In the violent style to which they were accustomed, they stole them from their neighbors, the Sabines.

Just as Rome needed women to continue its growth and ensure the expansion of the city, today the Caliphate needs women to grow socially. A report from the IS-controlled town of Baiji states that militants went door to door asking about the numbers of married and unmarried women in the houses, terrifying residents. "'I told them that there were only two women in the house and both were married,' said Abu Lahid. 'They said that many of their mujahedin [fighters] were unmarried and wanted a wife. They insisted on coming into my house to look at the women's ID cards [which in Iraq show marital status].'"⁷¹

Interestingly, the war spurred by the rape of the Sabine women came to a halt thanks to the very victims, the women, who convinced their male relatives to make peace with their abductor-husbands. Similarly, in Raqqa, before the town was taken over by the Islamic State, women offered themselves as human shields to protect the city from rebel forces.⁷² Raqqa was a peripheral city composed of tribes who initially supported Assad's regime and subsequently switched loyalties to the Islamic State. It is the best example of how the Caliphate plans to run the new state by engaging with the local population. For example, it hopes to neutralize internal opposition by establishing blood relationships between the conquerors and the conquered, blood relations in the form of marriages between the Islamic State warriors and local Sunni women, which, in time, will cement consensus and provide legitimacy.

The Caliphate's Ultimate Challenge

The modernity and pragmatism of the Islamic State springs from a mix of contemporary tactics, technological and communication skills, psychological propaganda, old-style warfare, and tribal customs, such as arranged marriages between the women of Sunni tribes and the jihadists. Against this background, it is clear that the Islamic State has dwarfed all previous or contemporary shell-states in nation-building and that it may succeed where all post-war armed organizations have failed: to create out of sheer violence a new type of state, big enough, strong enough, and strategically important enough to command the world's attention. Indeed, it has already mobilized more nations than the G20 to fight it. The alternative to recognizing IS and the Caliphate, an outright war with foreign soldiers on the ground, would hurt more innocent civilians and completely destabilize the Middle East, while facing low odds of long-term success. Of course, in light of the announced US plan for a prolonged air strike campaign and of the formation of a grand coalition, such a war cannot be ruled out.

Is it possible that one day European heads of state will shake hands with al Baghdadi? However repugnant this thought is today, the story of the rape of the Sabine women should remind us that anything is possible, providing there is sufficient consensus.

At the time of this writing, negotiating with the Islamic State is out of the question. But if Iraq is partitioned and IS manages to establish its own state in the Sunni areas in both Syria and Iraq, and from this stronghold move into Jordan, Lebanon, or other strategic areas of the region, things will look very different. Could the West, and indeed the world, permit a rogue state to exist at the gates of Europe and even closer to Israel? And is it possible that this shell-state, constructed through barbarous violence, will ever achieve the necessary legitimacy though internal consensus to transition into a modern state? If so, wouldn't it be better to bring such a state into the international community, thereby forcing it to respect international law, before it entirely redraws the map of the Middle East at our own disadvantage? The fear that the Gulf States show vis-à-vis the advancement of the Caliphate near their borders seems to point out the potential revolutionary force of IS in these countries.

It would not be the first time that a rogue state and rogue rulers have undergone such transition. Gadhafi, for example, was recognized in Libya. It would, however, be the first time in modern history that a state is born out of pure terrorism through a pre-modern war of conquest.

These are the exceptional challenges we face today. Regardless of how we approach them, the birth of the Caliphate reminds us that what politicians mistook for a new breed of terrorism may well turn out to be a new model of terrorism. That is, the Islamic State may break the mold and solve the dilemma of terrorism by succeeding in nation-building, granting members of an armed organization the status of enemies and civilian populations the status of citizens. Even without diplomatic recognition, the simple fact of the Caliphate's existence would change the way the international community looks at terrorism.

How likely is this scenario? Is it any more so than it

might have been for any other modern armed organization at any other time? The Islamic State has assimilated some of the characteristics of the modern state, such as domestic legitimacy gained by a rough social contract, and learned how to apply its politics of manipulation to the advantage of its leadership. Ironically and paradoxically, to justify its claim to statehood, the Islamic State has created its own mythology from the ashes of the very one the US manufactured to de-legitimize the regime of Saddam Hussein: the myth of al Zarqawi.

Chapter Four

The Islamist Phoenix

In 2009, Abu Bakr al Baghdadi was released from Camp Bucca, a US detention camp in Iraq named for FDNY Fire Marshal Ronald Bucca, who died on September 11, 2001, responding to the World Trade Centre attacks. Though it is not clear why al Baghdadi was granted amnesty along with thousands of other detainees, it is likely that the Iraqi government, lacking resources to maintain the prison, emptied Camp Bucca as US troops readied to depart Iraq in 2010.

As he was leaving the camp, al Baghdadi quipped to the Long Island reservists escorting him out, "See you in New York."[73] At the time few paid any attention to his vow. When in late spring 2014 al Baghdadi became Caliph of the Islamic State, Army Colonel Kenneth King, former commanding officer of Camp Bucca, recalled the statement, now a chilling warning.[74]

With al Baghdadi's election as Caliph, King admitted his surprise that his former ward had become the world's most wanted terrorist. In captivity, al Baghdadi had not been considered a virulently extremist Sunni. Indeed, until weeks before the declaration of the Caliphate, few in the media had paid him or his group any attention. Of course this would not be the first time the US overlooked, out of sheer ignorance and bad planning, a formidable enemy. It is nonetheless astonishing that the entire world could have missed al Baghdadi's spectacular successes in Syria in 2012 and 2013, a time when the eyes of the world were trained precisely on that country.

It is equally disturbing that the future Caliph's astonishing achievements were made possible by stepping into the shoes of his globally notorious predecessor, Abu Musab al Zarqawi, whose myth of the superterrorist was itself manufactured by the Bush administration. Even more shocking is the fact that al Baghdadi borrowed from the Americans the instruments and techniques of propaganda that they had employed to construct and globally disseminate the terrifying, false mythology surrounding the Jordanian jihadi leader. Ironically, as Bush and Blair had, al Baghdadi held in mind a very ambitious goal, bigger than many could envisage: the redrawing of the map of the Middle East—in al Baghdadi's case the carving out of a new state, the Caliphate.

The Making of a Superterrorist

Contrary to what many believe, Abu Musab al Zarqawi's stardom in the jihadist firmament and his role as archenemy of the US is a classic example of self-fulfilling prophecy. When Colin Powell singled out al Zarqawi as al Qaeda's man in Iraq, the Jordanian became the new jihadist star almost overnight and sponsors started throwing money at him and his group. Not only there was no link between al Qaeda and Saddam Hussein, but also al Zarqawi was a very small fish in a large jihadist pond. Judging from the successes of the Islamic State, today this self-fulfilling prophecy has come back to haunt us.

The first time American authorities heard of al Zarqawi was toward the end of 2001, after 9/11, from the Kurdish secret services. The Kurds claimed that al Qaeda had funded a new base in Bajara, in Iraqi Kurdistan, which was run by a new jihadist organization, Ansar al Islam. In 2001, Jund al Islam, a group of Jordanians from the City of Salt who had met al Zarqawi while he was imprisoned in Jordan and had remained in touch with him, merged into Ansar al Islam.[75] Without hard evidence, the Kurdish secret service used this alliance to link al Zarqawi to al Qaeda. Al Zarqawi was singled out as the go-between for both groups because of his personal contacts with the Jordanians and his Afghan camp in Herat, located on a popular jihadist route from northern Iraq to Afghanistan.

The Americans knew nothing about al Zarqawi, so they immediately contacted the Jordanian authorities to find out more. It was at this point that in Washington the idea of constructing a mythology around him as justification for the intervention in Iraq began taking shape.

Joint US and Jordanian investigations accused al Zarqawi of having masterminded a foiled al Qaeda plot in Jordan during the millennium celebrations, as well as the assassinations, in 2001, of an Israeli citizen, Yitzhak Snir, and, in 2002, of the American diplomat Lawrence Foley, for which an unknown armed organization, the Honorables of Jordan, had claimed responsibility. No hard evidence was produced to back such charges. Indeed, at the end of April 2004, after al Zarqawi was sentenced to death in absentia for both assassinations, the Honorables of Jordan released a statement denying any involvement by him. The message was accompanied by the shell casings of the bullets that had been fired at Foley and Snir.[76]

The Americans had much to gain from the creation of his myth. From September 11, 2001, to March 20, 2003, the United States built its case for attacking Iraq. Saddam's regime was accused of possessing weapons of mass destruction and supporting terrorism. Without any proof of the existence of the former, Saddam's support for terrorism was the only trump card the US administration held to convince the world that the Iraqi dictator had to be removed. To play it, the administration needed to demonstrate what was untrue: that Saddam Hussein and al Qaeda were connected. Their fictitious link was Abu Musab al Zarqawi.

The Power of Social Media

The successful manufacturing of the myth of al Zarqawi rests on two factors: the power of the media, which spread across the globe a terrifying message delivered by Colin Powell to the UN Security Council, and the willingness of Western citizens to believe this dubious message in the aftermath of 9/11. Just over ten years later, the Islamic State has been using social media to spread a terrifying new and equally false set of myths. And, as it was a decade ago, the world seems well inclined to believe them.

Al Baghdadi and his followers understand the importance of virtual life and our tendency to act irrationally when dealing with mysterious, terrifying issues such as terrorism. Showing a clear understanding of sophisticated communications analysis, they have invested extraordinary energy in social media to spread frightening prophecies, in the knowledge that they will have self-fulfilling effect. They also seem perfectly conscious that in a world where the twenty-four-hour media cycle has turned journalists and readers into junkies of shocking and extraordinary events, the truth value of an account takes second place to its shock value.

As we have seen right from the beginning, when the first group of jihadists from the Islamic State in Iraq crossed over to Syria, the organization's goal was to carve out its own territorial stronghold. This was an ambitious plan that it was believed could not be achieved without the spreading of a carefully crafted mythology to present al Baghdadi and his followers as a much stronger force than they were. A skillful, technologically savvy propaganda machine circulated false news of their exceptional strength through social media, a tactic that proved to be instrumental to their recruitment, fundraising, and military training programs. Indeed, as early as 2011 the organization attracted experienced fighters from Bosnia and Chechnya, people with outstanding military knowledge, who were not interested in joining any of the other jihadist groups in Syria.[77] The smoke and mirrors that the propaganda created fooled everyone and hid the bleak reality that at the end of 2010 the Islamic State in Iraq was on the brink of extinction and the migration to Syria was its sole long shot at surviving.

Even today, inside and outside the Caliphate, the propaganda machine is constantly in motion, spreading myths among young people of an ever stronger and ever more successful army, both abroad and at home. In Raqqa, a Belgian jihadist and his young son traverse the city in a propaganda van answering questions about everything from social services to job hunting. The van is packed with CDs, music, videos, leaflets, photos, and literature.[78] We are witnessing a phenomenon as old as our world that Plato brilliantly explained in the myth of the cave: those imprisoned within see nothing but the shadows cast on the walls before them, which they thus regard as the whole of reality.

Unlike the Taliban, who shunned anything technological, the Islamic State's propaganda is a high-tech
operation run by professionals, including some highly
educated individuals from the West. When Twitter and
Facebook took down the IS video of the beheading of
James Foley, within a few hours the propaganda team had
restored access through Diaspora-hosted sites.[79] And the
Islamic State propaganda has proven very seductive for
potential jihadists, especially in the West. It bears asking
what the NSA is really doing, then, with the transcripts
of our phone calls and email, if they have been unable
to intercept the numerous communications of Westerners bound for the Caliphate and arrest these would-be
fighters. The recent discovery that as early as 2009 a close
link existed between young Muslims from Minnesota
(two of whom died fighting for the Caliphate) and the
Islamic State,[80] causes one to wonder how the NSA could
have missed such a link.

This black hole in intelligence is particularly puzzling
considering that the Islamic State employs plentiful elec-
tronic strategies to widely disseminate its message. Its use
of the *ad hoc* app is illustrative. "One of ISIS's more successful ventures is an Arabic-language Twitter app called
The Dawn of Glad Tidings, or just Dawn. The app, an official ISIS product promoted by its top users, is advertised
as a way to keep up on the latest news about the jihadi
group."[81]

As we have seen, IS is also very good at latching onto

world events to proselytize. "During the 2014 World Cup it used hashtags such as #Brazil2014, #ENG, #France and #WC2014. This tactic allowed it to access millions of World Cup Twitter searches in the hope that some readers would click on links to its propaganda material, in particular a video showing British and Australian jihadists trying to persuade other Western Muslims to join their ranks."[82]

A possible answer to this puzzle may be found in the nature of the Syrian conflict. As opposed to Libya or Iraq, the Islamic State in Syria presents the West with a diplomatic quandary. Would the West compromise its relationship with Russia or China, or its appeasement with Iran, for a country where Western interests are very limited or nonexistent? Until the summer of 2014 the answer was "no." Aid workers, journalists, and refugees confirm that the flow of foreign fighters into Northern Syria kept rising as world events evolved. "They came in waves. After the coup in Egypt, those who had believed in the Muslim Brotherhood arrived at the conclusion that in the end the fate of Arab nations is decided in the US and the moderates had no more arguments to use to fight for democracy. Another wave came after the attack at Abu Ghraib in July 2013, [including] many of the prisoners who escaped, came to Syria, and joined the various groups. The last wave came after the chemical attack of the twenty-first of August, 2013," explains Francesca Borri. Almost all the foreigners entered Northern Syria across the Turkish border, flying to the airport of Hatay. "At the border between Turkey and Syria there is carpet of airline tags from all over the world," remembers Borri who flew to Hatay several times, a pilgrimage that for many was their last journey.

Clearly, Turkish authorities knew what was happening on the border with Syria and, if they wanted, Western and Israeli intelligence could have monitored this phenomenon. But it was only when IS moved into Iraq that the West took an interest in the Syrian conflict and the Islamic State.

Even if IS presented a political hot potato, it is unclear why the Western intelligence community did not take more interest in al Baghdadi and his followers while the group was growing in Syria. It would have been very easy to penetrate their virtual community. Back in 2013, for example, ISIS members, sympathizers, and sponsors followed on social media the dispute between al Baghdadi and Jabhat al Nusra's emir Abu Mohammed al Golani after the merger of their groups. When al Baghdadi and Ayman al Zawahiri clashed over the right to fight in Syria and the right to demand allegiance from factions of Arab, foreign, and local fighters, the global jihadist community was invited to express its opinion. "That fight required, in addition to a show of military capability on the ground, the ability to sell ISIS's Sharia views by paying due attention to ideology when marketing the organization, as evidenced by the speeches and messages exchanged between

Golani, Baghdadi, and Zawahiri. Those exchanges were discussed on jihadist forums and social media sites to assess Baghdadi's legitimate right to lead."[83]

Nor were these debates of interest to the numerous think-tanks that have proliferated since 9/11 to study radicalization and terrorism. One would think that Islamic State members' extensive use of social media and the most up-to-date techniques and tools to proselytize and raise money would be a gift to these organizations. The *Atlantic* magazine, doing its own analysis of the Islamic State's social media strategy, discovered that IS received seventy-two retweets for every tweet it sends by "using an Arabic language Twitter account, @ActiveHashtags, which advertises the most popular hashtags to get its own material on the feed."[84] The opportunities to study al Baghdadi's group through its use of social media were plentiful, but no one in a position to alter policy was interested in taking them up.

Paradoxically, Western intelligence and mainstream media not only ignored the Islamic State's development for a couple of years, but, when they finally did show some interest, they began listening to the wrong people. This confirms the absolute lack of proper information regarding the Syrian conflict and IS in Northern Syria. The first victims are the journalists. "Between April and May 2014, I was getting ready to go back into Aleppo from Turkey. Western intelligence briefed me about what was happening during the battle of Aleppo between the forces of Assad and the rebels. They told me that the rebels were winning and that the regime of Assad was falling, so it was safe to travel along the road from the border to Aleppo. I was the first foreign journalist to cross the border and my driver and myself ended up driving along fifteen kilometers of front line. I do not know how we survived but we did. When I got back I told Western intelligence that the rebels had all gone and the city was in the hands of Assad, but they did not believe me, nor did the international press want to publish my story. Both the intelligence and the media kept saying that what they saw in Facebook and YouTube was different. We get different news from the rebels via social media, they said, telling us and showing pictures of their victory. The only paper that published my story was *Le Monde*."[85]

For us, Facebook, YouTube, Instagram are more real than the report of a freelance Italian woman willing to risk her life to find out the truth. And the Islamic State, as well as the rebels and other groups engaged in the bloody Syrian and Iraqi conflict know it.

The Final Seduction of the Caliphate

In 2003, the mainstream media disseminated the government-sponsored myth of al Zarqawi as a superterrorist without checking its authenticity. Ten years later, social media achieved a similar result, contributing to the spread and internalization of a deliberately inflated image of the power of al Baghdadi and of his armed organization. Just as happened ten years ago, nobody bothered verifying these claims. But propaganda and media are not enough to mobilize people if the illusion they project does not coincide with some dream or nightmare formulated by the collective imagination. We know that in the aftermath of 9/11 the world was deeply traumatized, so we can understand why it was easy for Bush and Blair to move public opinion based on lies. What is harder to comprehend, however, is the appeal of the Islamic State to its social media followers. We are talking about a considerable number of people. The Islamic State has reportedly attracted 12,000 foreign fighters, of whom 2,200 are from Europe.[86] These figures do not take into consideration supporters and sympathizers abroad. For example, while sixty Australians are estimated to be fighting in Syria and Iraq with the IS, the number of supporters at home is believed to be one hundred.[87]

What motivates young, professional Muslims born in the West to give up their lives and join a war of conquest in a land they do not even know, in a conflict reminiscent of those fought in the Middle Ages? What, in a word, is the final seduction of the Islamic State? These are the questions we should ask ourselves.

In part it is the opportunity to vindicate fellow Muslims in the Middle East from humiliation, but this was the case also for many Western suicide bombers after coalition forces invaded Iraq. Perhaps there is something more that motivates young Muslims to join this jihad. The opportunity to be part of the construction of a new political order in the Middle East, a modern state without racism or sectarian tension (after some ethnic cleansing, of course), presented an unparalleled opportunity. Could it be that followers of IS look forward to the Caliphate as an uncorrupted and incorruptible nation with a profound sense of brotherhood, a society without the challenge that Western and Westernized Muslim women pose to men, a nation ruled by honor, a contemporary society perfectly in harmony with *al Tawhid*, the mandate of God? Indeed, this idealistic nation not only promises Muslims deliverance from centuries of humiliation, it also represents a twenty-first-century Sunni political utopia, a powerful philosophical construct that for centuries scholars have tried to deliver, to no avail. This, indeed, is the modern political force that the West and the rest of world have chosen to ignore until the summer of 2014.

If this analysis is correct, the ultimate appeal of the Islamic State rests upon its ability to convince young Western professionals to embrace this utopia and the belief that the Caliphate has the power to implement it, as the Zionist movement in the 1940s rallied the global Jewish community around the utopia of a Jewish state and instilled in them the certainty that it could turn the dream of a modern Israel into a reality.

Unlike the early state of Israel, however, the Syrian and Iraqi populations do not welcome the presence of foreigners. "In the fall of 2012 the first foreigners started to arrive in Syria to participate in the civil war. The Syrians let them in because they needed all the help they could get but they were not happy about it and kept saying that as soon as the Assad regime would fall the foreigners would go back. But everybody knew that they would stay," recounts Francesca Borri.[88] "There is a lot of tension between the locals and the foreign fighters, who are the most brutal and violent. Because they have not experienced dictatorship and war like the locals, they mistrust journalists and harass them. I never had any problems with the Syrians, but I was threatened by a New Zealander who came into Syria working for a Western NGO infiltrated by the Islamic State."

Not all the fighters are motivated by the utopian dream of a new Muslim state. For many young Westerners, joining the jihad or the rebels is an adventure, a kind of military summer camp. These are the most dangerous, because they show no compassion for the local population and no understanding of the suffering endured by them.

The Modern Version of Salafism

In Syria, as well as in Iraq, the proficiency of al Baghdadi and his group at making Sunnis believe they might succeed where all others had failed is a feat remarkable for its modernity. In the past, no jihadist group had even been equipped to run a real state. They had no idea how to manage water supply, sewage, or road building, nor did they know how to exploit the virtual world to recruit and fundraise across the globe. They were further ignorant of how to build consensus within communities. These failures, which we have seen in Afghanistan with the Caliphate of Mullah Omar, rest on the pre-modern vision of society that radical Salafism has projected.

Though the dream of the jihadist movement has always been to recreate the Caliphate, this was nothing more than a vague, romantic idea, entirely inapplicable in modern times, as Salafism rejected the construction of the modern state. Radical Salafism, rather, had frozen the concept of the ideal society in its manifestation in seventh-century Arabia. All subsequent events are superfluous and dangerous, from the infrastructure of the modern state to modern technology, as evidenced by the Taliban's ban on music, radio, and TV.

Against this background, what al Baghdadi has done, carving the Islamic State in Iraq's own enclaves in Syria and running these communities as a political authority with all the instruments of the modern state, is truly exceptional. He has "fuse[d] the political Islamists' aim of seizing state power with the neo-traditionalists' more global vision to create a recognizable, if rough-edged, state that is simultaneously supposed to be a launch-pad for greater expansion. This unprecedented combination is a powerful one," writes Jason Burke, a veteran of the study of the jihad.[89]

The manufacturing of the myth of al Zarqawi proved successful because after 9/11 there was a desperate need to put more than one face to the atrocities committed by al Qaeda, and Saddam Hussein, a much-hated dictator, fit the profile. At the same time, Bush and Blair succeeded in lying to the world and to their own governments, who thought the possibility that they were being actively deceived inconceivable. World public opinion still clings to the absurd belief that in the modern nation state the daily battle of politics is between good and evil only. Those who had not fallen victim to this fantasy, however, knew that no link existed between al Qaeda and Saddam Hussein, and that invading Iraq would eventually destabilize the entire region.

Today these same people are denouncing the manufacturing of another absurd myth, not in the West but in the Muslim world: that of the Caliphate and its leader, al Baghdadi; they are also witnessing the unfolding of another self-fulfilling prophesy through the power of social media. After decades of war and destruction at the hands of the local elite, backed by Western powers, Sunni Arabs and Muslims desperately want to believe that finally, from the ashes of a world long gone, a magnificent phoenix has risen. That is, a state and a leader who will bring them their long-awaited deliverance from the hellish present. Is al Baghdadi that man, and is the Caliphate that state? The West and the world strongly believe that they are not, but only the people of the Middle East can deliver, in time, the correct answer.

Chapter Five

The Modern Jihad

The Islamic State's destabilization of the Middle East has made strange bedfellows of various regional powers and forces us to confront a series of uncanny scenarios: the Iranian and Saudi sponsorship of the Palestinians in their conflict with Israel over the summer of 2014; Iran and Saudi Arabia's secret meetings to discuss possibilities for dissolving the Caliphate; US covert operations to arm Syrian "rebels," comprised primarily of jihadist, not secular, elements; and President Obama's decision to bomb the Islamic State's strongholds in Syria with the backing of a grand coalition of Western and Arab states but no UN mandate, to name just a few. The most surprising development of all, however, is not found among these strange alliances, but rather in the staggeringly successful nation-building of these armed and seemingly backward insurgents, as compared with the dismal nation-building attempts of the United States.

The United States has been at war nearly continuously since Vietnam—for more than half a century. It has done so, in its own words, "to spread democracy." Following a repetitious cycle of wars varying from "full-scale invasions and occupations to counterinsurgency, proxy wars, and back again,"[90] the US military has produced less than encouraging results, especially in Iraq. How can we forget that the Americans captured and recaptured Mosul to annihilate the jihadists? They fought for Fallujah twice with heavy losses. Yet, when Bush and Blair's armies pulled out of Iraq, they came home "victorious."[91] At the time of this writing, however, both cities are under the rule of the Caliphate.

In sharp contrast to the US military, with its high-tech propaganda and seductive mythology, the Islamic State has waged a successful war of conquest using terrorist tactics—a war fought under the ideological banner of jihad, a holy war. If military superiority cannot guarantee victory, as the many US defeats of the last fifty years suggest, the key to military success must lie elsewhere. This warrants an examination of the motivations of the armies of the US and IS.

Both militaries justify their actions with an appeal to a larger cause. This begs the question: Is the promise of a radical Salafist state whose borders trace those of the ancient Caliphate a more powerful motivation than the will to "spread democracy," in the process incidentally paving the way for market colonization by Western multinationals? Judging from what we have seen in the last eleven years, the correct answer may well be yes. If al Baghdadi's holy war is indeed a more powerful motivator than the exportation of Western democracy, it becomes imperative to understand what type of conflict he is waging.

Two Jihads

Developed after the death of the Prophet Mohammed by the *Ulema* (the global community of Muslim religious scholars), *jihad* was an elaboration of the teachings of the Koran and of the Prophet. However, there are two types of jihad: the great jihad, which is mostly spiritual, that is, the daily fight of each individual against his or her temptations; and the small jihad, the physical fight against an enemy. What interests us here is this latter type, whose concept has evolved through the centuries, while the great jihad has remained unchanged.

Formulated when Islam was already a superpower, the idea of the small jihad reflected an imperial spirit. It was a tool to protect the community of believers. Religious scholars of this period further distinguish two forms of small jihad: defensive and offensive. The former was the obligation of all members of the community to take up arms against the enemy to safeguard Islam. The offensive jihad, on the other hand, could be called only by the Caliph, the ruler of the community. Its task was to spread Islam, not to protect it. The jihad that the Islamic State is waging falls into both of these categories.

As long as the Caliph had sufficient warriors ready for

combat, the citizen was exempt from being drafted in the offensive jihad. But when more soldiers were needed, no true Muslim could ignore the call of their spiritual and political leader. This principle is still in place today. Thus, al Baghdadi, as the legitimate successor of the Prophet Mohammed, not only has the right to wage wars of conquest, but can demand the participation of all Muslims in these conflicts, as well as demand their migration to the Caliphate. "Those who can immigrate to the Islamic State should immigrate, as immigration to the house of Islam is a duty,"[92] al Baghdadi declared in his proclamation of the Caliphate.

It follows that the advent of the modern Caliphate undermines the authority of any other jihadist organizations or rulers. Potentially, the Islamic State represents a challenge to the legitimacy of all Muslim governments, because it imposes the authority of the Caliph on them.[93] This claim should not be dismissed when assessing the type of threat that the Caliphate poses, both to Muslims and to the rest of the world. Indeed, one of the tasks of the grand coalition that President Obama promoted under the umbrella of NATO, with the active participation of several Muslim states, in September 2014, is to prevent the Islamic State's further territorial expansion in the region.

In jihadist chat rooms and Twitter messages, supporters of the Islamic State maintain that the US and the British strategy of not negotiating for the release of their hostages, who they know will be beheaded, is aimed at stirring up public fear. Once incited, such fear may create a domestic political climate that supports military action, as happened in 2003. Only this time, the attack would aim to protect Western allies in the region, namely the Saudis and other Gulf state elites, from the revolutionary message of Caliphate, which could indeed stir a revolution inside these nations.

As imperial Islam faded, the "small jihad" assumed new meanings, adapted to the needs of the time. Faced with the uncompromising violence of the Franks in the Second Crusade, Saladin, the Abuyyid Sultan of Egypt and Syria, redefined the concept of small jihad.[94] The radical spiritual resources of Islam animated his followers in their successful campaign of re-conquest.

At the beginning of the twentieth century, the memory of Saladin's jihad became part of the Middle Eastern struggle for independence from the colonial powers of Europe. During the British domination of Egypt, Hassan al Banna, the founder of the Muslim Brotherhood, reshaped the jihad into an anti-colonial conflict, a fight for full independence from the British. A few decades later, Sayyed Qutb, an Egyptian intellectual, transformed it into a revolution, a vehicle for regime change.[95]

Since the late 1950s, the debate over the true meaning of modern jihad has revolved around three defining concepts: counter-Crusade, anti-colonial struggle, and revolution. The Islamic State seems to have incorporated all of these characteristics to give the small jihad an entirely new meaning: that is, nation-building. "Rush oh Muslims to your state," al Baghdadi declared in his inaugural address as Caliph. "It is your state . . . This is my advice to you. If you hold to it you will conquer Rome and own the world, if Allah wills."[96]

The counter-Crusade against Western culture and interests in the Middle East, as expressed through the alliance between corrupted Muslim elites and Western powers, prepared the ground for the traditional war of conquest waged by al Baghdadi. Nation-building in the conquered territories also requires regime change— hence the revolutionary nature of al Baghdadi's fight in Syria and Iraq, countries ruled by corrupted elites at the service of foreign powers. But what makes this modern jihad particularly powerful among Muslims is the fact that it has, in a relatively short time, actually succeeded in achieving some measure of nation-building.

The Geography of Jihad

Al Qaeda has accomplished nothing close to the birth of the Caliphate, and has never actively engaged in nation-building. Rather, its leadership was too busy plotting to attack America. "Al Qaeda is an organization and we are a state," explained an Islamic State fighter, who gave his name as Abu Omar, in an online chat with the *New York Times*.[97] This statement perfectly summarizes the different roles that the two armed groups play in the eyes of many Muslims and the distinctive challenge that each poses to the world.

According to this analysis, 9/11 was a punch in the face of the West, while the establishment of the Caliphate is a knock-out blow to its key Middle Eastern allies, a blow that threatens the very existence of a geopolitical order originally designed to benefit the west and its oligarchic friendly elites. This may come as a surprise to Westerners, but it should not surprise those who rule the Middle East. Soon after 9/11, the head of Saudi General Intelligence told the man in charge of the British Secret Intelligence Service, the MI6, Sir Richard Dearlove, "9/11 is a mere pinprick on the West. In the medium term, it is nothing more than a series of personal tragedies. What these terrorists want is to destroy the House of Saud and remake the Middle East."[98] Dearlove, then, was presented with a chilling prophecy that the Islamic State is attempting to prove true.

It was only a matter of time before a jihadist armed organization would challenge the Middle Eastern establishment, reformulating ancient concepts in modern terms. Only a matter of time before an armed group would flesh out the ultimate Muslim utopia, the new Caliphate, and present it to millions of Sunnis as a feasible plan of action using the tools of modern propaganda. In the eyes of many Muslims, the Islamic State, like its predecessors, is nothing more than the product of decades of abuse, corruption, and injustice. But unlike its predecessors, IS has adapted to a newly multipolar geopolitical environment and undertaken a pragmatic approach to the populations living in its territory.

The sensitivity to domestic issues, as well as its endogenous characteristics, are equally part of the appeal that the Islamic State exercises. In sharp contrast, al Qaeda has always been perceived as a foreign power, something that al Badhdadi attempted to avoid when in 2010 he changed the name of his group from al Qaeda in Iraq back to the Islamic State in Iraq. Indeed, when al Qaeda came to be resented in the Middle East, it was not because the organization was run by a Saudi billionaire and an Egyptian intellectual, both totally removed from the day to day lives of most Muslims, but rather because the organization had chosen to take the jihad out of the Middle East.

It is unquestionable that the events of 9/11 opened up a second front, against the far away enemy, the United States, away from the refugee camps, out of the daily suffering of the Middle Eastern people and away from the injustice that the corrupted Arab regimes perpetrated upon them. Moreover, 9/11 was an attack that few within the jihadist community approved. Lodged in the heart of the US with the intent to weaken America's power and deprive the ruling oligarchies of the Middle East of its support, the attack, in the Western media, came to symbolize the jihad. Though some in the Middle East cheered at the collapse of the Twin Towers, the regional consensus had in fact been that nothing good could come of such tactics. On the contrary, taking the fight so far away might have disastrous consequences at home. And indeed it did.

In retrospect, the absurdity of attacking the far away enemy is obvious. But Osama bin Laden had the means to mastermind 9/11 at a time when other jihadists could barely make ends meet. Today, things are very different. While the Islamic State runs the Caliphate on the historical soil of Islam, the historical nucleus of al Qaeda has been destroyed. Bin Laden is dead, and the organization he founded has been reduced to a generic jihadist logo.

Al Baghdadi's nation-building effort in Syria and Iraq is a powerful draw in part because of where it is located. Geography has always been essential for Islam, both religiously and politically. In a CNN documentary, a smuggler of foreign fighters across the Southern Turkish border near Hatay explains what some of these men feel when entering Syria. "For many, the crossing itself is a religious experience. When they get to the fence, they kneel and cry, they weep, like they've just met something more precious to them than their own family. They believe this land, Syria, is where God's judgment will come to pass."[99]

The cultural impact of the old Caliphate upon the territory it controlled was massive, to the extent that today, centuries after the disintegration of this splendid culture, a common language across the Middle East and North Africa still exists. Equally, the fall of the Caliphate spurred centuries of conquest and humiliation, and carved deep scars in the identity and self-esteem of the Muslim population. When the Europeans redrew the map of this historic and ancient territory, these wounds reopened. Time and time again, since the eleventh century, every movement of Muslim rebirth has nurtured the deeply nostalgic dream of recreating the old boundaries of the Caliphate, as if recomposing its geography could magically recreate its splendor.

Geography is also at the root of the most recent radicalization of the Salafist movement, out of which both al Baghdadi's and al Zarqawi's visions of jihad took shape. What triggered this radicalization was the signing of a peace agreement between the Jordanian government and Israel in 1994, regarded by many as an extraordinary event. The agreement represents the official acknowledgement of the geographical right of Israel to exist in a land considered part of the Caliphate. Its signing was a watershed for the jihadist movement, triggering the birth of a new wave of clandestine Salafist organizations, among them the Jordanian al Tawhid.

Chapter Six

Radical Salafism

The root causes of what we are witnessing today trace back to the extraordinary political event that Salafists regard as the ultimate betrayal: the acceptance by Arab statesmen of Israel as a political power on Muslim soil, in the ancient territory of the Caliphate.

Founded with similar motivations across the Arab world in the early 1990s by veterans of the anti-Soviet jihad organizations such as the Groupe Islamique Armé (GIA) in Algeria and the Aden-Abyan Islamic Army in Yemen, al Tawhid, the group of which Musab at Zarqawi was first a member, is a radical Salafist organization nearly identical to the others. All of these armed groups share the same objective: to ignite a revolutionary jihad throughout the Muslim world and oust pro-Western governments. This civil war, or *fitna*, would evict the existing Arab regimes, which Salafists regard as *taghut* (idolatrous).[100] After joining the group in prison, al Zarqawi went on to become its emir. Thus, when he formed his armed organization in Iraq he chose the name al Tawhid al Jihad. That both al Zarqawi and al Baghdadi share the Salafist creed—

al Baghdadi hailing from a religious Salafist family—was key to the compatibility of their visions of jihad.[101]

At its outset, however, during the second half of the nineteenth century, Salafism was not an anti-Western ideology. On the contrary, it was Arab admiration for the modernized West that gave birth to the movement. Fascinated by European development, Arab countries began to compare their socioeconomic and political conditions with those of Europe. This evaluation triggered a deep reflection on the crisis of the Ottoman Empire, the political power that controlled the Arab world at the time, and stimulated great interest in Western civilization. In the Arab world this process is known as al Nahda, literally, the "awakening" or "renaissance." Produced by the interaction of Arab thinkers with Western revolutionary ideals, al Nahda marked the beginning of Arab modernization or, rather, of the will to modernize. In essence, the Arab world acknowledged the socioeconomic and political superiority of the parliamentary European states. Looking to the achievements of the old Continent, Arabs wanted to create a Muslim modernity in the new Arab states emerging from the disintegration of the Ottoman Empire emulating Western political culture.[102] This was a time in which the construction of the nation state greatly appealed to progressive Muslims.

Salafism, therefore, has always sought to modernize the Arab world, and it has identified the Ottoman Empire as the primary cause of the Arab failure to develop as Europe did. To overcome this obstacle, the Salafist doctrine called for all Muslims to go back to the purity of religion, to the origins of Islam and the teachings of the Prophet. In short, Salafism stressed the need to reconnect with one's roots as a means of creating Arab identity, which would in turn provide the necessary strength to gain independence from the Ottoman Empire. This was essentially a process of spiritual purification, of cleansing, after centuries of political and economic domination.

Towards the end of the nineteenth century, however, betrayal by European powers, whose contribution to the modernization of the Arab world came in the form of brutal colonization, catalyzed Salafism's transformation into a xenophobic and puritanical revivalist movement. The central goal of modern Salafism is still the purification of Islam, now from the contamination of corruption and stagnation produced by Western colonization. Foreign European powers, not the Ottoman Empire, are blamed for the decline of the Arab world; hence, the rejection of the nation state and of European modernity.

Against this religious and philosophical background, in the 1950s, Sayyed Qutb reformulated the concept of *Tawhid*,[103] the divine and absolute unity of God, to give it a distinct political identity. "God is the source of power," wrote Qutb from the Egyptian jail where Nasser had imprisoned him, "not the people, not the party, neither any human being."[104] This notion, known as *al hakimiyya lil-llah* (the principle of the government of God), projects a political Islam and its sole successful expression (the Caliphate) into the core of the political arena, the boundaries of which are strictly defined by the interpretation of the Prophet's teachings, not by modern forms of government such as democracy or socialism.

As such, Qutb's message is one of total severance from the Western-style politics embraced by Nasser and, at the same time, an exhortation to cleanse Islam of any external influence, sacred or profane. Any departure from the principle of the government of God, Qutb affirms, is an act of apostasy (*riddah*).

Although the accusation of apostasy (*takfir*) is originally a religious concept, it has, over Islam's history, been molded into a powerful political weapon. It allowed Qutb, an Arab, to challenge the political legitimacy of Nasser, another Arab, painting him as an infidel on par with the Western colonizers. In power struggles within Islam, the accusation of apostasy is common. The first instigated by a *takfir* was fought soon after the death of the Prophet, during the reign of Caliph Abu Bakr (632–34), and is the genesis of the schism between Sunnis and Shias.[105]

Through the centuries, both Sunnis and Shias have used the concept of *takfir* to exclude each other from power. As we shall see in the following chapter, in recent times both al Zarqawi and al Baghdadi have used *takfir* to legitimize their genocidal wars against the Shias, whom they regard as the close and constant allies of foreign powers.

Chapter Seven

The New Mongols

In June 2014, global public opinion was shocked and disgusted at the news that after conquering Mosul, the army of the Islamic State turned against Shia women and children in nearby villages. Using machine guns, they killed hundreds of innocents, dumping the bodies in mass graves. They looted Shia homes and confiscated Shia property. In the town of Tal Afar, for example, al Baghdadi's warriors confiscated 4,000 houses as "spoils of war."[106] They bombed and burned shrines and mosques with the intent to wipe away all sign of Shia presence in their territory. This type of destruction has been repeated in every corner of the Caliphate to implement the religious cleansing that many believe the most radical interpretation of Salafism demands.

As we shall see, however, the bloody sectarian civil war that the Islamic State has initiated has less to do with the radical doctrine of Salafism and more with the use of genocidal warfare as a tactic to gain control of the insurgency, a strategy that al Zarqawi engineered in 2003, soon after coalition forces invaded Iraq.

Whatever the aim of these heinous acts, the word genocide seems well suited to describe what has been happening in recent years in Syria and, since the beginning of the summer of 2014, in Iraq. Indeed, today, to be a Shia or a member of a related sect, such as the Syrian Alawati, comes very close to being a Jew in Nazi Germany. Following in al Zarqawi's footsteps, the Islamic State appears inclined to eradicate the Shia population from the Caliphate by any means possible, including extermination.

Against this backdrop, many believe that al Baghdadi's involvement in Syria in 2011 had nothing to do with the removal of the Assad regime, but rather was motivated by a desire to ethnically cleanse the Alawati from the region destined to become the cradle of the new Caliphate. Again, the parallel with Nazi Germany and the supremacy of the Aryan race cannot be avoided. While Hitler justified the extermination of the Jews with a fictive eugenics, the Islamic State uses the concept of takfir, apostasy, to carry out the religious "purification" of Islam. Shias, and the followers of all creeds but Salafism, are heretics guilty of a sin so serious as to demand death.

Before exploring the true motivations for this genocide, it is imperative to understand the power that the concept of *tafkir* exercises in the collective imaginations of both Shias and Sunnis.

Al Takfir

The genesis of *takfir* can be traced back to the first violent clash between the Sunnis and Shias, the Great Fitna, the first civil war among Muslims. Ignited in 655 AD, a year before the assassination of Caliph Uthman, this feud broke when the followers of Mohammed fought over the issue of succession. Uthman was charged with apostasy by the supporters of Ali, who claimed that Ali was the direct descendent of the Prophet, hence he should be Caliph. The Great Fitna gave birth to the schism between the Shias, the followers of Ali, and the Sunnis, the followers of Uthman. Ever since, each of these two branches of Islam has accused the other of apostasy, of *takfir*, in its respective bids for political power.[107]

Since the seventh century, the concept of takfir has remained solidly anchored to political and economic issues. Possibly, because the Prophet was both a religious and a political leader, the boundaries between the material and spiritual domain within Islam were blurred from the start. Hence *takfir* became an instrument, a tool of politics dressed in religious garb. In the eighteenth century, for example, Abd al Wahhab, a Saudi preacher and the founder of the Wahhabi movement, accused the Ottoman Empire of apostasy; he claimed that it had departed from the true source of legitimacy, the word of God. The accusation of *takfir* that Wahhab launched at the Turks allowed the House of Saud to take up arms against its rulers, the Ottomans in the Arabian Peninsula.[108] For the next two centuries, the war of conquest conducted by two powerful allies, the House of Saud and the Wahhabists, was fought with economic and political weaponry dressed up as religious zeal.

Defining *takfir*, much like defining *terrorism*, has always been slippery, and this explains why the concept represents a powerful tool in the hands of Muslim armed organizations and sectarian powers to justify their claim to legitimacy. As we have seen in previous chapters, in the 1950s and 1960s members of the Muslim Brotherhood reformulated it to justify their opposition to Nasser, whom they claimed had pushed them into the underworld of illegality, a case of Sunnis employing *takfir* as a weapon against other Sunnis

Originally, the final aim of *takfir* was not the exclusion of heretics from the spiritual community, nor their extermination, but rather their eviction from the material community: removing them from the system of social rights and privileges and from the economy. Hence, they were pushed outside the boundaries of political legitimacy. The concept of the extermination of the Shias was not introduced until 2003 when al Zarqawi launched several suicide attacks against Shia targets.

The Blindness of the West

The first such suicide mission in Iraq took place on August 29, 2003, targeting the Imam Ali Mosque in

Najaf. This event represented a watershed in the Iraqi conflict, opening a second front against the Shia population.
It had already been justified by a propaganda campaign
launched months before and bankrolled by key Sunni
players in the region, including Saudi Arabia and several oligarchs from the Gulf states. The Iraqi Shias were
accused of having forged alliances with foreign powers
seeking a regime change in Iraq, acts that Salafists considered *mukaffir*, or grounds for *takfir*.

Using a timeless, apocalyptic rhetoric, a parallel was
drawn between the forthcoming invasion of Iraq and the
thirteenth-century invasion of the Mongols. Images of Mongols and Tartars sacking the splendid city of Baghdad in 1258
are, for Sunni Iraqis, evocative of shameful memories.[109]

Soon after the fall of Saddam's regime, a vast literature
became available on the internet about the new Mongol
invasion. In the virtual magazine *Bashaer*, the reader
learned that, before reaching Baghdad, the Mongols had
invaded the kingdom of Khwarizm (in today's Uzbekistan
and Turkmenistan), just as Coalition forces had attacked
Afghanistan before invading Iraq.[110] Mongols and Tartars
forged an alliance to wage war against Baghdad, as had the
United States and the United Kingdom. In both circumstances, Baghdad was attacked from the east and west, the
siege lasted twenty-one days, the military superiority of the
invaders was enormous, and people were so afraid that they
did not pray on the first Friday after the attack had begun.
In the thirteenth century, as in modern Iraq, the rivalry

between Shiite and Sunni weakened central power. Mongols and Tartars advanced with armies of mercenaries who participated in the invasion and sacked the city; Coalition forces stood by as their Iraqi supporters looted libraries and cultural institutions and killed women and children.

Bashaer's analogy ends with a prediction drawn from the historical close of the Mongol invasion: two years after the sacking of Baghdad, the Syrian and Egyptian armies, together with groups of Arab volunteers, defeated the Mongols and the Tartars at Ayn Jalut. "We are sure that God will punish America for good," the editorial concludes. "When will the new Ayn Jalut take place?"[111] Today the Islamic State is carving out its Caliphate, having launched its offensive from Syria. In so doing it hopes to build toward a contemporary Ayn Jalut.

In the summer of 2003, al Zarqawi used the analogy of the Mongol invasion to justifiy his offensive against the Shia. As al Zarqawi explained it, Ibn al Alqami, the Shia vizier of Baghdad, had helped the Mongols in their conquest of the city, urging his followers to do the same.[112] In a similar fashion, the Shias had conspired with the Americans and welcomed them into Iraq. This was the first time that sectarian infighting between Sunnis and Shias surfaced within the Iraqi insurgency.

The attack in Najaf, which marked the beginning of al Zarqawi's active fight against the Shias in Iraq, represents the first manifestation of the clash between Sunnis and Shias, a civil war that the Islamic State still carries on. As

al Zarqawi explained to bin Laden in a rich correspond-
ence from 2003 to 2005, the *fitna* against the Shias was
only a tactic to prevent the formation of a united secular
front against Coalition forces from which the jihadist
would be excluded, similar to the one that decades earlier had led the Iraqi struggle for independence from the
United Kingdom.[113]

But in 2003, Coalition forces had failed to appre-
ciate the significance of a war between Sunnis and
Shias—a serious oversight. At the time, the motives for
the bombing seemed incomprehensible, its perpetrators
unknown. In the summer of 2003, Coalition forces were
battling al Sadr's militia—considered the primary armed
opposition in Iraq. At that time, the Sunni insurgency,
composed primarily of remnants of the Baath party and
Muslim nationalists, did not pose a serious threat. Yet a
close look at how Islamic radicalization had advanced in
Iraq during the economic sanctions would have offered
useful clues to the fact that a major civil and sectarian war
was brewing, with the potential to destabilize the entire
Muslim world.[114]

The West had not paid attention to the profound changes
that swept over in Iraq during the economic sanctions
of the 1990s. Under the patronage of Saddam Hussein,
modern Salafism had taken hold across Iraq, and become a
source of powerful radicalization. The new religious fervor
of the Iraqi dictator aimed at appeasing the Sunni tribes in
times of great economic difficulties. During the UN eco-

nomic sanctions, religion had become a source of comfort for the impoverished Sunni middle class, the backbone of Saddam's regime, and Islam a spiritual means of coping with prolonged economic hardship. At the same time, the radicalization of Iraq helped Saddam hide the economic failures of his regime. For example, by prohibiting women from working in public places and subsequently even at home, he quickly halved unemployment.

Unlike Western powers, jihadists knew that for a decade many in the Sunni Triangle had been harboring radical Salafist religious beliefs. Hence, soon after Saddam's fall, they flocked to this area from all over the Middle East. Some were even linked to local Iraqi Salafist groups, all based inside the Sunni Triangle in places like Ramadi, Fallujah, and Mosul, which became prime breeding grounds for the jihadist Sunni insurgency. Al Zarqawi was among these new arrivals.

Much as Coalition forces had virtually ignored the changes that a decade of economic sanctions had produced in Iraq, those same nations ignored too the danger that the proliferation of jihadist and insurgent groups in Syria, bankrolled by Gulf sponsors, posed to the entire region. The West and the world conveniently dismissed the radicalization of Iraq and Syria as a product of religious fanaticism.

The Religious Alibi

It is surreal that Western powers believed that what is taking place in the Middle East is a war of religion motivated by a feud started in seventh-century Arabia. Indeed, when similar conflicts have been waged by Christians, religion has rarely been more than a pretext for politics. In fifteenth-century Europe, apostasy was a crime that commanded a gruesome death by fire. Europe was alight with the auto-da-fé, as bodies were burned in the name of God. Today, the Caliphate uses decapitation and crucifixion in a similar fashion.

The greatest danger faced by fifteenth-century Europe was the possibility of a civil war between Catholics and Protestants, one fought along religious lines, but with roots in the Continent's ancient, vicious power struggles. Today, the accusation of apostasy, or *takfir*, against the Shiite population aims at triggering just such a civil war (*fitna*) in Iraq, Syria and beyond—that is, a war which at first glance appears to be motivated by religion, in which political and economic interests are obscured. But as in fifteenth-century Europe, the true motivations are political and economic and their roots are found in the power struggle to control the entire region.

The Caliphate is well aware that to build a new state, and to construct legitimacy through consensus, much more than a sleek campaign of religious propaganda promulgated on social media is needed. In particular, cleansing its territory of Shias from its territory offers many advantages for nation-building, guaranteeing the support of local Sunni populations, producing a more homogeneous populace with fewer opportunities for sectarianism, and freeing up resources to offer fighters as spoils of war. In a word, the extermination of the Shias makes things easier for the leadership of the Caliphate both economically and politically, while at the same time satisfying a deeply rooted desire for revenge among the Sunnis, which can only help build consensus within and loyalty to the new state.

The warfare, therefore, far from reflecting a religious mission, is in fact a political tactic implemented by a highly pragmatic leadership. Unlike the Taliban or the Nazis, the Islamic State shows flexibility: those willing to convert are welcomed into the new state, while those able to pay the *jizyah*, a tax linked to their heresy, can leave freely. The Caliphate is even willing to release hostages to foreign powers for ransoms.

Pragmatism springs from the hard task of nation-building, which is the Islamic State's top priority. To successfully rule regions plagued by decades of war requires a complete reconstruction of all socio-economic infrastructures, keeping foreign Arab interests at bay while waging a war of conquest. More than a functioning religious alibi, what is most needed is a steady and large flow of money.

The Islamic State has transcended the mythology and

rhetoric of previous jihadist groups. It has shown pragmatism and modernity in developing the strategies required to pursue its ambitious dream of nation-building. It has privatized the business of terrorism very quickly, gaining independence from its sponsors and establishing an economics not entirely dependent upon war. It has created partnerships with local Sunni tribes to quell opposition and share revenues generated by the exploitation of key resources. It has been circumspect, even clever—something we cannot say of the Assad or Maliki regime.

Chapter Eight

Contemporary Pre-Modern Wars

Since June of 2014, world leaders have been battling the rising power of the Islamic State. We have seen them presenting their electorates with plans for dealing with the threat, laden with novel terminology. And IS has responded—at some times with acts of barbarity, such as the beheadings of James Foley and Steven Sotloff, and at others through statements made by European IS members and hostages like John Cantlie.[115]

How did an armed organization, virtually unknown just three years ago, come to challenge the world's greatest powers? Not only militarily, on the battlefields of Syria and Iraq, but ideologically, using all the modern means of communication?

The answer lies in the progressive breakdown of the nation state in Syria and Iraq. Emptied of their role as representatives of their populations, these nations' governments regressed to the conditions of pre-modern enclaves.

The Disembodiment of Arab Nations

In Syria, the Arab Spring met with a violent response and, amid the indifference of the world, a dream of democracy collapsed. This was brilliantly summarized by Ali Khedery, who served as special assistant to five American ambassadors in Iraq and as senior adviser to three heads of US Central Command from 2003 to 2010. "Facing Assad's army and intelligence services, Lebanon's Hezbollah, Iraq's Shia Islamist militias and their grand patron, Iran's Revolutionary Guards, Syria's initially peaceful protesters quickly became disenchanted, disillusioned and disenfranchised—and then radicalised and violently militant."[116]

Sectarian fronts opened almost overnight and peaceful protests morphed into a civil war, which in turn degenerated into a modern proxy war, with several rich Gulf states bankrolling their own Sunni armed groups in pursuit of revenge against Iran, their number one Shia enemy, and Assad, Tehran's Arab ally. Many of the international rules of war were broken, including prohibitions on the use of chemical weapons against civilians, and the wealthiest villas in Aleppo were looted. In the blink of an eye, a twenty-first century nation was riven by seemingly intractable conflict.

In Iraq, Nouri al Maliki, ignoring his promises to share power with other political groups, consolidated it instead, through a sectarian campaign aimed at destroying his rivals. He attempted to arrest his vice-president, Tariq al

Hashimi, "supported by Iran and armed with US-made Humvees, M-16s, and M1A1 tanks."[117] The same ordeal was reserved for a second prominent Sunni rival, the finance minister Rafea al-Essawi, who abandoned politics and fled to his tribe's stronghold in Iraq's Anbar province.[118]

"Facing mass unrest, Iraq's Sunni Arab provincial councils voted for semi-autonomous rule like that of the neighboring Kurdistan region. Maliki blocked the implementation of a referendum through bureaucratic ploys, in contravention of Iraq's constitution. Demonstrations of civil disobedience erupted across the Sunni provinces, as millions of Iraqis once again saw that they had no stake in Iraq's success—only its failure. Claiming intelligence that al Qaeda had penetrated the protest camps, Maliki crushed them with lethal force. Several dozen people were killed during an Iraqi military raid in Hawija in April 2013, further inflaming what were already spiking sectarian tensions."[119]

Two Shia leaders, Assad backed by Russia and al Maliki backed by the West, abused their power and violently repressed the call of the people for true democracy. Both leaders reneged on their promises. Assuming power after the death of his father, Assad had inflamed mass hope with the promise democratic reforms. Similarly, al Maliki had pledged to rule according to the constitution and to preside over Iraq's first truly democratic government.

Iraq is the mirror image of Syria, backsliding into pre-modernity. Damascus leads by a few years in this depressing process; the disintegration of the Iraqi state has only just begun. And the Islamic State has shown an extraordinary understanding of the similarities between the countries, exploiting them with remarkable timing.

Will the West and the world deal with Iraq differently than they have with Syria, especially now that the Islamic State has proclaimed its Caliphate? This is a question that nobody can answer. In the past, neither the US nor Europe could find a formula to overcome Russia and China's veto on any military intervention in Syria. While everybody knows that Assad guarantees the Russian fleet access in the Mediterranean, China's reluctance springs from how badly the Europeans and the Americans have handled regime change in Libya, leaving a profoundly unstable country. And after the lies Bush and Blair used to justify their invasion of Iraq, and the high price paid by Coalition forces, the West is in no rush to topple another Arab dictator.

The current policy of containment in Syria may prove insufficient when faced with an armed organization that has morphed into a state. Indeed, the nature of the challenge that the Islamic State poses is very different from the one presented by conflicts in areas where the modern state has collapsed.

World War III

In the summer of 2014, Pope Francis declared that World War III had already started, a miasma of conflicts spreading across the globe, bearing little resemblance to the two world wars of the twentieth century. Instead, these conflicts are reminiscent of pre-modern warfare, managed not by sovereign states but by warlords, terrorists, militias, and mercenaries, whose ultimate goal is territorial conquest with the aim of exploiting people and natural resources. None of these wars are waged to create nation states.

Missing are the trenches, battlefields, and even international rules that to some extent used to set codes and boundaries for the behavior of combatants. The Geneva Convention has been consigned to the trash bin. The parties to these various conflicts are all guilty of severe excesses, including religious violence, wanton destruction, and even genocide. Even some regular armies behave as militias. In Nigeria, Amnesty International has filmed Nigerian soldiers and members of the Civilian Join Task Force, a civilian militia, cutting the throats of prisoners suspected of membership in the notorious Islamist militia Boko Haram, and throwing the decapitated bodies into mass graves.[120]

From Nigeria to Syria, from the Sahel to Afghanistan, the victims of this new war are largely civilians. In Nigeria, according to estimates by Amnesty International, 4,000 people, mostly civilians, have been killed in attacks carried out by Boko Haram and the Nigerian army in the past year. In Syria more than one million people have been displaced, and 200,000 have been murdered, since the beginning of the civil war.

Similar statistics can be gathered at the edges of the European Union. From April to August 2014, the UN estimates that 1,129 civilians have died in violent clashes between the Ukrainian National Army and separatist, pro-Russian militias. Other unofficial statistics report a much higher figure.

What we face are pre-modern conflicts that harness modern technology, a deadly combination that hugely increases civilian casualties. One striking example is the shooting down of Malaysian Airlines Flight 17 in July 2014 over Ukrainian airspace.

Professor Mary Kaldor of the London School of Economics, author of *New and Old Wars: Organized Violence in a Global Era*[121] has written that globalization plunges some regions into conditions of anarchy similar to philosopher Thomas Hobbes's famous description the state of nature: "The state of men without civil society (which state we may properly call the state of nature) is nothing else but a mere war of all against all . . . with a continual fear and danger of violent death." Life before civil society was "nasty, brutish and short." These are the conditions into which parts of Syria and Iraq have regressed today.

Globalization has undermined the stability of a number of authoritarian regimes, from Libya to Syria to Iraq and beyond, by making people aware of their political conditions. The fall of Gaddafi in 2011 resulted in a political vacuum that rival tribal militias—from liberals to hard-line Islamists—have filled with violence. The violent responses to the Syrian Arab Spring and the Sunni Iraqi uprising have created a similar vacuum. The common objective of the many armed groups that have filled it is the conquest of political and economic power for the purposes of exploitation. These groups harbor no intention of creating a democratic state, nor a new nation in any modern sense of that term. On the contrary, anarchy is the best environment for the pillaging of resources and exploitation of people.

The process of the state's degeneration and collapse is therefore the root cause of the pre-modern nature of today's conflicts, and is a phenomenon increasingly tied to economic factors—to the drastic impoverishment of large regions and populations.

Globalization has brought prosperity in some regions, such as China and Brazil, and poverty in many others, such as the Middle East and parts of Africa. The crisis of the state in Africa is linked to both climate change and the race of rich countries to grab the continent's resources. In the Middle East, other phenomena have contributed to this impoverishment. In Iraq, for example, a decade of economic sanctions has transformed the nation with the highest level of education in the Arab world to one in which women do not have the right to work. The process of regression to a pre-modern society has gone hand in hand with the nation's impoverishment.

The deadly combination of globalization and rising poverty has stirred up widespread insecurity and fostered tribal armed conflicts under the banners of religion and faction. Conflicts have inevitably become multipolar. In Mali, Tuareg separatists and Islamic factions are fighting amongst themselves and at the same time against the government; in the Central African Republic, Muslim and Christian militias are involved in a bloody war, which threatens to become genocide, while members of the national army take positions according to their creeds; in Western Africa, al Qaeda in the Maghreb is active almost everywhere.

Brutal violence characterizes all of these conflicts—often on camera. The most striking example is the killing of the American journalist James Foley by the Islamic State; the video of his beheading quickly made the global circuit of social media.

However, it would be misguided to lump the Islamic Caliphate's war of conquest in Syria and Iraq in the same category with the pre-modern conflicts described above. Though the war of conquest that IS is waging is part of Pope Francis's World War III, it differs fundamentally from the contemporary pre-modern conflict that other armed groups are waging.

Redefining the Modern State

The Islamic State shares in the ambitious goals of the founders of the European nation state, articulating these goals in a contemporary and modern way. Like Israel's,

IS's concept of a nation state is ethno-religious, rather than solely ethnic. It also attempts to fulfill all the requirements of the modern state: territoriality, sovereignty (for now recognized only internally), legitimacy, and bureaucracy. Instead of being satisfied with small enclaves, it seeks to create a twenty-first century version of the ancient Caliphate and shuns the idea of permanent anarchy. On the contrary, in the conquered territories, one of the first tasks that IS carries out is the imposition of Sharia law.

The Caliphate considers the maintenance of law and order to be its responsibility, and implements them, if in a rough and rudimentary manner. The Caliphate is also responsible for the protection of the areas under its command from enemy attack. Hence, the Islamic State also takes up the task of national security. Law and order and national security are the two key indications that distinguish a modern state from a pre-modern enclave run by war lords and barons. The other important element is the consensus of the population, what Rousseau defined as the social contract, its legitimacy.

There is no doubt that the Islamic State aims to establish consensus by any possible means. Unlike other armed groups, for example, it is using the revenues from strategic resources, like oil wells and hydro-electric dams, not only to bankroll a war of conquest but also to rebuild key socio-economic infrastructure inside the Caliphate.

Sophisticated propaganda is committed to promoting the image of a real state, legitimized by the Muslim population, not only locally but also internationally. Abu

Bakr al Baghdadi is presented to the entire community of Muslims, the Umma, as the new Caliph, a descendant of the Prophet Mohammed. The Caliphate spreads images of a regular army, quite different from the armed gangs of al Qaeda or Boko Haram, an army that is fighting traditional battles on fields and in trenches, using modern weapons (ironically, for the most part American and Russian, stolen from the Iraqi and Syrian army respectively). It recruits internationally with sophisticated propaganda; its foreign soldiers come from Europe, the US, Asia, North Africa, Australia, and even New Zealand. While it may be engaged in sectarian cleansing, the Caliphate is missionary and offers anyone the opportunity to convert to Sunni Salafism and thus become a citizen. Those who refuse and cannot flee are executed. It negotiates with foreign powers for the release of hostages, showing a pragmatism that al Qaeda never has.

Where the Islamic State differs from the modern nation state is in the means used to achieve this geographical and political construction: terrorism. While revolutions are regarded as an acceptable source of legitimacy for the modern state, terrorism is not.

Amid the existential crisis of modern democracies in a multipolar world, and in the midst of the destabilization of the Middle East, against the background of a World War III reminiscent of pre-modern conflicts, the true challenge of the Islamic State rests on its nascent efforts at nation-building. Regardless of whether the Caliphate succeeds in establishing itself as a new state in the near future, the new model with which it has experimented will inevitably inspire other armed groups. The failure of the West and the world to address this issue will have devastating consequences for the world order.

EPILOGUE

During the writing of this book, while the Islamic State was setting the Middle East on fire, the Umbrella Revolution—yet another uprising of young people crying for democracy—paralyzed Hong Kong. Are these event somehow related? And what is the link between the Arab Spring and a brutal terrorist organization that has successfully morphed into a state and is redrawing in blood the map of the Middle East?

The democratic uprisings of the last decade and the Islamic State are both products of the current multipolar world disorder, a phenomenon that has been taking shape since the end of the Cold War. The Arab Spring and the Islamic State, in particular, are a modern Janus head, two responses to the same problem: a corrupt middle eastern leadership. Why is the latter successful where the former has failed?

As we have seen, the Islamic State presents not just a new breed of terrorism, but a truly modern phenomenon. Could this be the main source of its success? It is possible. While the West and its Muslim allies refused to acknowledge the advent of a new international political landscape, the Islamic State has not only adapted, but has fully exploited it.

The emergence of a multipolar system, where the power of the United States is kept in check by rising powers overseas like China, has made older models of foreign policy obsolete. Western intervention in Syria under a UN mandate remains improbable because of China's and Russia's opposition. But even with the ostensible legitimacy of the grand coalition assembled by President Obama, intervention against the Islamic State will be limited to Iraq and confined to aerial bombing in support of local troops. In other words, the coalition will back anybody willing to fight the Islamic State on the ground, broadening the already huge diameter of the modern war by proxy. This approach risks encouraging other groups to follow the path of the Islamic State and use the arms and the money supplied by their sponsors to carve out their own states, further destabilizing the Middle East.

The American and European decision to arm the Peshmerga and the PKK, still listed as terrorist organizations, has already redrawn the battle lines in the fight for an independent Kurdistan in Turkey, a nation where 20 percent of the population is of Kurdish origin. Violent clashes between the Kurds and the Turks have already broken out in several Turkish towns, and demonstrations in favor of an independent Kurdistan have been staged all over Europe. Among these was a brief occupation of the European parliament.

Meanwhile the question of military intervention continues to baffle Coalition forces. Aerial bombing seems insufficient to stop the advance of the Islamic State's army; hence the question of whether to redeploy ground troops to Iraq may soon come up for debate. Whatever the outcome, it is clear that foreign intervention will not halt the destabilization of the region—it never has and it never will—and that a fresh and more pragmatic approach is badly needed to prevent further deaths and destruction. This approach must acknowledge the existence of a new power in the region and must recognize that war by proxy is a strategy doomed to boomerang. Accordingly it must seek to address this new power using instruments other than war.

The emergence of this multipolar system has opened novel opportunities for those who understand the new rules of the game. We have seen how the Islamic State has exploited the Syrian war by proxy to its own advantage, and how it is exposing,, through its powerful propaganda machine, the surreal contradictions of Obama's grand coalition.

As well as modern politics, the Islamic State has mastered modern technology to proselytize, recruit, and raise money, and this is a clear sign of modernity. The nation-building successes of its digital campaign offer a textbook example of the power of communication. The same cannot be said of the several democratic protest movements of the last decade.

The Iranian street uprising of 2009 was fueled by Twitter. In 2011 the Arab Spring's use of Facebook made what was happening in Cairo visible to the world. A year later the Occupy movement broadcasted its protests on YouTube. Today, the Umbrella Revolution in Hong Kong is using Bluetooth to bypass Internet censorship. Yet none of these movements has brought about political, economic, and social changes of the magnitude of those achieved by the Islamic State.

Modern technology and a clear understanding of how our multipolar world functions, however, are not enough to succeed. Is it possible that the "smartphone uprisings," including the Arab Spring, failed where the Islamic State has succeeded because the latter is managed by a professional elite, which guides the rank and file, while the former finds itself at the mercy of their constant interaction and participation? If so, is the Islamic State's model of nation-building more modern than that of the Arab Spring? This are frightful questions that democracies and legitimate states must address if they want to prevent the proliferation of a new wave of authoritarianism.

Is there a third option besides the failure of the Arab Spring and the successes of the Islamic State? Yes, there is, and it involves education, knowledge, and an understanding of the changing political environment we live in—the same instruments used in the past to bring about political change without bloodshed but with consensus, something that both the young warriors of the smartphone and the gray suits of politics still fail to understand.

GLOSSARY

Alawati: A religious sect in Syria that follows a mystical brand of Shia Islam. As they have historically kept their beliefs secret from outsiders, not much is known about them; they hold a significant minority in Syria, with believers comprising 12 percent of the population.

Anti-Soviet jihad: The war fought by Afghan and other Muslim warriors (mujahedin) against the Soviet invasion and occupation of Afghanistan from December 1979 to February 1989. Ended with the defeat and withdrawal of the Soviet Army.

Sheik Abdullah Azzam: A Sunni Muslim who spoke in support of jihad against the Soviet invaders during the late 1980s. Along with bin Laden, he established the Afghan Services Bureau, which raised funds and recruited terrorists, and al Qaeda. He was killed by a car bomb in November 1989.

Abu Bakr al Baghdadi: The leader of ISIS and self-proclaimed Caliph of the Islamic State.

Caliph: Title of the chief Muslim civil and religious ruler who protects the integrity of the state and the faith. The Caliphs are regarded as the successors of Mohammed. The term derives from the Arabic *khalifa*, meaning "successor." "Caliph" was also the honorary title adopted by the Ottoman sultans in the sixteenth century, after Sultan Mehmed II conquered Syria and Palestine, made Egypt a satellite of the Ottoman Empire, and was recognized as the guardian of the holy cities of Mecca and Medina.

Caliphate: The dominion or rule of the Caliph.

Crusades: A series of military campaigns fought by Christian armies from Western Europe to reclaim the Holy Land from Muslim control. In 1095, Pope Urban II launched the First Crusade. Between the eleventh and thirteenth centuries there were eight Crusades, and the knights who took part in them believed that they were assured of a place in heaven. For Muslims, the Crusades were a sustained military campaign to expand the territory of Christendom and eliminate Islam.

Euskadi ta Askatasuna (ETA): Euskadi ta Askatasuna, which means "Basque Fatherland and Liberty" in the Basque language, is an armed group fighting for the independence of the Basque country from Spain. ETA originates from the EKIN, a nationalist group that changed its name to the Euskadi ta Askatasuna in 1958. The group's initial activities involved planting explosives in Basque cities such as Bilbao. In 1968 ETA put its first military initiative into action, and in subsequent years it intensified its violence targeting security forces and politicians. The group is still active in Spain and maintains ties with armed groups all over the world. Its membership is believed to be quite small, perhaps no more than twenty hardcore activists and several hundred supporters, and its headquarters are believed to be in the Basque provinces of Spain and France.

FARC: Founded in 1964 by Manuel Marulanda Vélez and other members of the Central Committee of the Communist Party of Colombia (Partido Comunista de Colombia—PCC), the FARC (Fuerzas Armadas Revolucionarias de Colombia, in English, "Revolutionary Armed Forces of Colombia") is an armed organization with a Marxist bent whose aim is to overthrow the government. It claims to defend the rural poor against Colombia's wealthy classes and therefore opposes American influence in Colombia, the privatization of natural resources, and the presence of multinational corporations. The group targets wealthy landowners, foreign tourists, and prominent international and domestic officials. It is structured in a military fashion and its members, estimated at around 7,000, wear uniforms and behave as a regular army. Its importance has grown thanks to an alliance with Colombian drug traffickers. Experts estimate that the FARC takes in between $200 million and $400 million annually—at least half from the illegal drug trade. The rest is generated through kidnappings, extortion schemes, and an unofficial "tax" levied in the countryside (www.contrast.org/mirrors/farc/).

Fitna: Originally considered a trial of a believer's faith, *fitna* now refers to periods of unrest and internal war within the Muslim community. It is often used in Islamic history with the specific sense of civil war.

Groupe Islamique Armè (GIA): An Islamist armed group believed to have been founded in March 1992 by Arab-Afghans who, returning to Algeria after the Afghan war. It is headed by the emir Abou Abd Ahmed, also known as "Djafaar al Afghani." The GIA's final aim is to overthrow the country's current military-backed government and establish an Islamist state based on Sharia. Its membership is estimated at around 20,000–25,000. Since December 1993, the GIA has carried out particularly violent attacks against foreigners in Algeria as well as against Algerian citizens.

Hamas: Created on December 14, 1987, (five days after the beginning of the Intifada) as a Palestinian branch of the Muslim Brotherhood, the group's objective is to establish an Islamic Palestinian state in place of Israel. The PLO's main rival in the territories occupied by Israel, Hamas benefited from Yasser Arafat's failures on the international front, especially after the Gulf War. It considers war the only means to free the Occupied Territories, and has established a direct link between Islam and the liberation of the Occupied Territories that limits, or even excludes, all compromises on the issue. It is responsible for many attacks in Israel, primarily suicide bombings, but was prepared to recognize Israel as a condition of joining a coalition government in the early summer of 2014. Its activities are concentrated in the Gaza Strip and a few areas in the West Bank. Hamas's objectives as stated in its charter of August 18, 1988, include, in addition to the liberation of Palestine and the creation of an Islamic Palestinian state, the rejection of any Western presence in Muslim countries and opposition to the secularization and Westernization of Arab society.

Hezbollah: Arabic for "Party of God," Hezbollah is a radical Lebanese Shia group formed in 1982 in response to the Israeli invasion of Lebanon. It advocates the establishment of Islamic rule in Lebanon as happened in Iran, the liberation of all occupied Arab lands, and the expulsion of non-Muslims from Muslim countries. The group is sponsored by Iran and predominantly operates in the Bekaa Valley, south of Beirut. Its membership is estimated at 40,000 in Lebanon and several thousand supporters. It possesses heavy artillery such as multiple BM-21 rockets. A number of its members are known or suspected to have been involved in numerous armed attacks against the US. Hezbollah also goes by the name of Islamic

Jihad, but its official armed wing is called the Islamic Resistance. The latter, created in 1983, oversees military operations in south Lebanon. It has 400 well-trained fighters and 5,000 supporters. Besides sporadic attacks (mostly bombings and murders), it leads proper military operations against the Israeli and Lebanese armies. Militarily organized, the Islamic Resistance's activities have become increasingly illegal since 1993. The group has tried especially to establish a popular base in south Lebanon through social aid activities, such as its Jihad al Hoed ("Holy effort for the reconstruction"), which finances the reconstruction of buildings destroyed by the Israeli army. It also gives $25,000 to the families of the "martyrs" who die during its suicide operations.

Imam: In general use, it means the leader of Muslim congregational prayers, a post that requires no ordination or special spiritual powers beyond sufficient education to carry out this function. It is also used figuratively by many Sunni Muslims to refer to the leader of the Islamic community. Among Shiites the word takes on many complex meanings. In general, however, and particularly when capitalized, it indicates to Shias the descendant of the Party of Ali believed to have been the designated repository of God's spiritual authority.

Islamism: A political ideology based on the belief that Muslim religious principles should dominate every aspect of public and private life.

ISI: Islamic State in Iraq.

ISIS: Islamic State in Iraq and Syria. Also known as Islamic State of Iraq and the Levant (ISIL) and the Islamic State (IS), this terrorist organization was officially created in 2013, though its history stretches back to the early 2000s and al Qaeda. Its territory covers large swaths of both Iraq and Syria, and its forces were attacking the Iraqi city of Mosul as late as early September 2014.

Jabhat al Nusra: a branch of al Qaeda that operates in Syria and Lebanon. They were created in 2012 during the Syrian Civil War. They have had several clashes with ISIS, and as of the printing of this book were losing badly in open warfare with the Islamic State.

Jihad: This term has often been mistranslated as "Holy War," a concept coined in Europe during the Crusades. "Jihad" is Arabic for "striving," and a better translation of its meaning as a religious doctrine would be "striving in the cause of God." There are two aspects of jihad: great jihad, the struggle to overcome carnal desires and evil inclinations, and small jihad, the armed defense of Islam against aggressors. The term has been used by different armed groups in their violent confrontations with the West; famously, Osama bin Laden called for a jihad in his fatwa against Americans, calling for "just war" against the oppressor.

Jizyah: a tax enacted on sections of Islamic societies who are not Muslims. While the tax is not upheld by nation-states in the Islamic world, IS enforces it in some areas.

Koran: The holy scripture of Islam.

Kufr: Literally "disbelief," the term is used to describe those who do not believe in Islam.

Modern Salafism: Radical interpretation of Salafism. A

strongly anti-Western movement that calls for a return to the purity of Islam.

Mujahedin: Plural form of the Arabic word *mujahed,* literally meaning "one who makes jihad." The term was applied to Muslims fighting the Soviet occupation of Afghanistan (1979–89), and has been translated as "holy warriors."

Muktab al Kidmat: Also known as the Arab-Afghan Bureau. An organization founded in 1984 by Osama bin Laden and Abdullah Azzam. Its purpose was to raise funds and recruit terrorist soldiers against the Soviets. After Azzam's death in 1989, Muktab al Kidmat was absorbed into al Qaeda.

Muslim Brotherhood: Founded in Egypt in 1928, this association is considered the prototype for all modern Islamist movements of Sunni obedience. Present all over the world, the Muslim Brotherhood promotes a reformist Islam.

Al Nahda: A cultural renaissance occurring during the late nineteenth and early twentieth centuries in Egypt and the larger Middle East, spurred on, among other factors, by contact with Europe. It is seen as a period of intellectual modernization and reform.

Nationalism: Term used to describe the sentiment and ideology of attachment to a nation and to its interests. The word originates from the theory that a state should be founded in a nation and that a nation should be constituted as a state. Nationalism requires the consciousness of national identity, which may include territorial integrity, common language, shared customs, and other elements of culture.

Mullah Omar: The spiritual leader and commander of the Taliban. He was also Afghanistan's leader from 1996 to 2001, and was deposed when the United States invaded the country.

Ottoman Empire: The Muslim empire established at the end of the thirteenth century by Osman I, founder of a Turkish dynasty in northwestern Anatolia, and enlarged by his successors, known as the Ottomans, who took over the Byzantine territories of western Anatolia and southeastern Europe. At its height, Ottoman power extended throughout the Middle East, parts of North Africa, and southeastern Europe, but the empire began to disintegrate in the nineteenth century and collapsed at the end of the World War I; the Anatolian heartland became the Republic of Turkey, and the outlying provinces were recognized as independent states.

Palestine Liberation Organization (PLO): A Palestinian nationalist movement and the central organization of all Palestinian movements, the PLO was created in 1964 by Ahmed Shukeiry under the auspices of Egypt. Its objective, as stated in its charter established in May 1964, is the creation of an independent Palestinian State on the territory today covered by Israel or, at least, in the Occupied Territories (Gaza and the West Bank). Its leader was Yasser Arafat from 1969 until his death in 2004, when he was succeeded Mahmoud Abbas, who continues to hold the post.

Peshmerga: Official name of the Kurdish Army. These fighters have existed in one form or another since the Kurdish independence movement of the 1920s, after the collapse of the Ottoman Empire, and notably include women in their ranks.

Al Qaeda: Literally meaning "the base," it was originally formed around 1988 by Osama bin Laden and Abu Ubaydah al Banshiri, bin Laden's top military commander, as a network to connect the Arabs who volunteered to fight in the anti-Soviet Jihad. Al Qaeda also helped to finance, recruit, and train Sunni Islamic extremists for the Afghan resistance. Soon, it became a multiethnic Sunni Islamist insurgent organization that remained active well beyond the end of the Afghan war. Its primary aim is the establishment of a pan-Islamist Caliphate throughout the Muslim world, and therefore it seeks the collaboration of other Islamist armed organizations to overthrow existing regimes regarded as "non-Islamic" and to expel Westerners and non-Muslims from Muslim countries. In 1998, it merged with the Egyptian Islamic Jihad ("al Jihad"). Its membership is thought to be anywhere between several hundred and several thousand people.

Red Brigades: The Red Brigades (Brigate Rosse, or BR) was formed in 1969 in Italy out of the student and workers' movements. Its ideology advocated violence in the service of class warfare and revolution. The group was based in and operated from Italy and mainly targeted symbols of the establishment such as industrialists, politicians, and businessmen.

Moqtada al Sadr: A deeply influential Iraqi Islamist leader. In February 2014 he suddenly withdrew from government.

Salafism: A sect of Islam that espouses strict, literal adherence to the tenets of Islam. Originating in the nineteenth century in response to European influence in the region, Salafism is sometimes considered puritanical, and often associated with jihad. Salafists are mostly located in Saudi

Arabia, Qatar, and the United Arab Emirates, and are considered to be the "dominant minority" in the Middle East.

SCIRI: Islamic Supreme Council of Iraq, an Iraqi Shia Islamist political party.

Sharia: Literally "legislation," a word that refers to the moral and legal code that binds religious Muslims.

Shiites: The lineage of the supporters of Ali, Mohammed's son-in-law, who refused to submit to Caliph Muawiyah in the Great Fitna, thereby creating the greatest schism in Islam.

Shell-state: The result of the process through which an armed organization assembles the socioeconomic infrastructure (taxation, employment services, etc.) of a state without the political one (i.e., no territory, no self-determination).

Sunnism: The largest sect of Islam. After Mohammed's death, those followers who supported a traditional method of election based on community agreement became known as Sunnis; they were opposed by the Shiites, who favored a hereditary transition in leadership.

Takfir: An accusation of apostasy.

Tawhid: The unity of God in Muslim theology.

Al Tawhid al Jihad: A militant Islamist group founded in Fallujah in 2003 and headed by Abu Musab al Zarqawi. The group arranged false documents for more than one hundred al Qaeda fighters who escaped from Afghanistan during the 2001 war. It also provided them with funds and a safe haven (near Tehran), and then organized their movement out of Iran to other areas in the Middle East and the West. In 2004, the group declared fealty to Osama bin Laden and changed its name to al Qaeda in Iraq. The name means "Monotheism and Jihad."

War by proxy: A term denoting third parties' fighting in place of larger world powers. A prime example of this type of warfare is the Vietnam conflict in the late 1960s and early 1970s.

Ulema: Islamic scholars.

Umma: The community of believers, which transcends national, ethnic, political, and economic differences.

Zakat: The obligatory almsgiving that constitutes one of the five pillars of Islam. Literally, "purifying."

Abu Mussab al Zarqawi: Islamic militant from Jordan who ran a terrorist training camp there in the mid-1990s. He rose to fame after going to Iraq and being responsible for a number of bombings during the Iraq War. Killed in 2006 by US forces.

ACKNOWLEDGMENTS

The process of writing this book began in June 2014 as I watched the latest incarnation of al Zarqawi's armed organization advance across Iraq. With my agent, Diana Finch, and my publisher, Dan Simon of Seven Stories Press, I re-read *Insurgent Iraq* and, examining the materials it gathered, concluded that my theories had been correct. So we began working as events exploded into the international consciousness, turning the Islamic State into the new archenemy of the world. And as we go to press, the situation continues to evolve.

Special thanks go to journalist and friend Laura Passetti, who helped me in gathering information and data on the Islamic State; to Edith Champagne, who showed me just how advanced is the media campaign conducted by the Islamic State; to Francesca Borri, who opened my eyes about the Syrian conflict. Ria Julien, a friend and the editor of *Insurgent Iraq*, again agreed to edit *The Islamist Phoenix*; so a special thank you goes to her for making my English better and clearer.

As usual, my assistant Federico Bastiani has been a valuable support; without him I would not have completed this work in time. A special thank you goes to my sister-in-law, Claudia Gerson, and to my dearest friend, Bart Stevens, for reading the manuscript, not once but twice. To Sally Klein, for cooking and looking after me while I wrote; and to her beautiful grandchildren for making me smile.

Thank you to Steven and Eleonora Creaturo for lending me their home in East Quogue where I edited the first draft.

Without the staff at Seven Stories you would not be reading this book, and without the work of Silvia Stramenga, its many translations would not be available.

A special thank you goes to Luigi Bernabó, my Italian agent, who never doubted that it would be a success.

Thank you to my husband, my children, my mother, and my aunt, who are always very supportive; to my cousin Marina and Davide; to my friends who, with their usual dependability, have listened to my endless theories about the Islamic State.

NOTES

1. Basma Atassi, "Iraqi Al-Qaeda Chief Rejects Zawahiri's Orders," http://www
.aljazeera.com/news/middleeast/2013/06/2013615172217827810.html

2. "Caliphate" is the name given to an Islamic state led by a supreme religious and
political leader known as caliph, or successor to the Prophet Mohammed. Of
the succession of Muslim empires described as "caliphates," the most famous
is the Ottoman Caliphate (or Empire) that ruled from 1453 to 1924. Centering
on the power of Turkish sultans, the Ottoman Caliphate expanded to cover the
Balkans and Hungary under Suleiman the Magnificent in the sixteenth century,
and reached the gates of Vienna.

3. Nick Paton Walsh, Gul Tuysuz, Raja Razek, "Al Qaeda-Linked Group
Strengthens Hold in Northern Syria," http://edition.cnn.com/2013/11/05/
world/europe/syria-turkey-al-qaeda/

4. To be modern implies a manner of apprehending the world that seizes upon its
present possibilities and dynamics of change toward fuller development. Paul
Nadal, "What Is Modernity?" http://belate.wordpress.com/2013/03/03/what-is
-modernity/

5. Various, "Life Under ISIS For Residents of Raqqa: Is This Really A Caliphate
Worse Than Death?" http://www.independent.co.uk/news/world/middle-east/
life-under-isis-for-residents-of-raqqa-is-this-really-a-caliphate-worse-than
-death-9715799.html

6. Hannah Strange, "Islamic State Leader Abu Bakr al-Baghdadi Addresses
Muslims in Mosul," http://www.telegraph.co.uk/news/worldnews/middleeast/
iraq/10948480/Islamic-State-leader-Abu-Bakr-al-Baghdadi-addresses-Muslims
-in-Mosul.html

7. Roula Khalaf, "Abu Bakr al-Baghdad: Isis Leader." http://www.ft.com/cms/s/0/
ec63d94c-02b0-11e4-a68d-00144feab7de.html

8. Paul Gilbert, *Terrorism, Security and Nationality* (London: Routledge, 1995).

9. Benoît Faucon, Ayla Albayrak, "Islamic State Funds Push Into Syria and Iraq
with Labyrinthine Oil-Smuggling Operation." http://online.wsj.com/articles/
islamic-state-funds-push-into-syria-and-iraq-with-labyrinthine-oil-smuggling
-operation-1410826325.

10. Alex Bilger, "ISIS Annual Reports Reveal a Metrics-Driven Military Command,"
http://www.understandingwar.org/sites/default/files/ISWBackgrounder_ISIS_
Annual_Reports_0.pdf.

11.   GPO, "PLO's Ability to Help Palestinian Authority Is Not Clear," http://www.gpo.gov/fdsys/pkg/GAOREPORTS-NSIAD-96-23/html/GAOREPORTS-NSIAD-96-23.htm.

12.   Press Release, "Islamic State Has Up To $2 Billion for the War Against the US," http://vestnikkavkaza.net/news/politics/60124.html.

13.   At the heart of the disintegration of the 350,000-strong Iraqi armed forces when ISIS attacked Tikrit and Mosul in June 2014, one finds more than cowardice and lack of loyalty. One also finds widespread corruption. Commanders drew salaries for "ghost battalions" that didn't exist, receiving money for 600 soldiers when in fact there were only 200. "Despite the vast expenditure on the army, said to total $41.6 billion in the past three years, units were sent to the front short of ammunition with only four magazines for each assault rifle. ISIS produced chilling videos showing the ease with which its snipers could wound and kill soldiers." http://www.independent.co.uk/news/world/middle-east/isis-caliphate-has -baghdad-worried-because-it-will-appeal-to-angry-young-sunnis-9574393.html.

14.   For all the rhetoric of the War on Terror as ushering in a new age of American imperialism, even in Iraq the West has not conquered new territories with the conceit of integrating them into its nation, as in a pre-modern war of conquest.

15.   John Gray, "A Point of View: Isis and what it means to be modern," http://www .bbc.com/news/magazine-28246732

16.   Lawrence Joffe, "Obituary: Ayatollah Mohammad Bakir al-Hakim." http://www .theguardian.com/news/2003/aug/30/guardianobituaries.iraq.

17.   David Rose, "Heads in the Sand," http://www.vanityfair.com/politics/features/2009/05/iraqi-insurgents200905

18.   Greg Bruno, "The Role of the 'Sons of Iraq' In Improving Security," http://www.washingtonpost.com/wp-dyn/content/article/2008/04/28/AR2008042801120.html

19.   Matt Bradley and Ali A. Nabhan, "Iraqi Officer Takes Dark turn to al-Qaeda," http://online.wsj.com/news/articles/SB10001424052702304834704579405440767359448.

20.   Bill Roggio, "Analysis: ISIS, allies reviving 'Baghdad belts' battle plan," http://www.longwarjournal.org/archives/2014/06/analysis_isis_allies.php.

21.   Ibid.

22.   Ibid.

23.   Ibid.

24.   The White House, "President's Address to the Nation, January 10, 2007." http://georgewbush-whitehouse.archives.gov/news/releases/2007/01/20070110-7.html.

25.   Peter Beaumont, "Abu Bakr al-Baghdadi: The ISIS Chief With the Ambition to Take Over al Qaeda," http://www.theguardian.com/world/2014/jun/12/baghdadi-abu-bakr-iraq-isis-mosul-jihad.

26.   Various, "Interior Published a New Picture of the Leader of 'Daash' Abu Bakr al-Baghdadi," http://www.shafaaq.com/sh2/index.php/news/iraq-news/71597--qq- .html (in Arabic).

27.   Jenna McLaughlin, "Was Iraq's Top Terrorist Radicalized at a US Run Prison?" http://www.motherjones.com/politics/2014/07/was-camp-bucca-pressure -cooker-extremism.

28. Various, "The biography of Sheikh Abu Bakr al-Baghadadi," https://archive.org/stream/TheBiographyOfSheikhAbuBakrAlBaghdadi/The%20biography%20of%20Sheikh%20Abu%20Bakr%20Al-Baghdadi_djvu.txt.

29. Lizzie Dearden, "Iraq Crisis: ISIS Leader Pictured for the First Time After Declaring Islamic Caliphate," http://www.independent.co.uk/news/world/middle-east/iraq-crisis-isis-leader-pictured-for-first-time-after-declaring-islamic-caliphate-9586787.html.

30. Sohrab Ahmari, "Inside the Mind of the Western Jihadist," http://online.wsj.com/articles/sohrab-ahmari-inside-the-mind-of-the-western-jihadist-1409352541.

31. Interview with Michael Przedlacki, September 16, 2014.

32. Aryn Baker, "Why Al Qaeda Kicked Out Its Deadly Syrian Franchise," http://time.com/3469/why-al-qaeda-kicked-out-its-deadly-syria-franchise/.

33. Paul Crompton, "The Rise of the New Caliph, ISIS Chief Abu Bakr al-Baghdadi," http://english.alarabiya.net/en/perspective/profiles/2014/06/30/The-rise-of-the-new-caliph-ISIS-chief-Abu-Bakr-al-Baghdadi.html.

34. Donald Neff, "The First Intifada Erupts, Forcing Israel to Recognize Palestinians." http://www.ampalestine.org/index.php/history/the-intifadas/364-the-first-intifada-erupts-forcing-israel-to-recognize-palestinians.

35. Loretta Napoleoni, *Terror Incorporated* (New York: Seven Stories Press, 2005).

36. Hannah Allam, "Records Show How Iraqi Extremists Withstood US Anti-terror Efforts," http://www.mcclatchydc.com/2014/06/23/231223/records-show-how-iraqi-extremists.html.

37. Bernard Haykel, "The Enemy of My Enemy Is Still My Enemy," http://www.nytimes.com/ref/opinion/26haykel.html.

38. Aryn Baker, "Syrian Rebels Appear to Have a new Type of US Made Anti-Tank Weapon," http://time.com/57313/syrian-rebels-are-seen-with-u-s-made-weapons/.

39. Erika Solomon, Daniel Dombey, "PKK 'terrorists' Crucial to Fight Against ISIS," http://www.ft.com/cms/s/0/4a6e5b90-2460-11e4-be8e-00144feabdc0.html#axzz3ATSuW000.

40. Interview with Francesca Borri, September 15, 2014.

41. Interview with a former Syrian rebel, August 10, 2014.

42. Interview with Francesca Borri, September 15, 2014.

43. "Opposizione siriana, Qatar ha pagato riscatto di 20 milioni di dollari per rilascio caschi blu da al-Nusra," *La Repubblica*, September 13, 2014 (in Italian).

44. "Il Fatto Quotidiano. Isis, nuovo video. L'ostaggio John Cantlie ai media: 'Dite la verità su Stato Islamico,'" http://www.ilfattoquotidiano.it/2014/09/18/isis-nuovo-video-lostaggio-john-cantlie-ai-media-dite-la-verita-sullo-stato-islamico/1125414/ (in Italian).

45. Elliot Ackerman, "Watching ISIS Flourish Where We Once Fought," http://www.newyorker.com/news/news-desk/watching-isis-flourish-where-we-once-fought

46. "ISIS Leader al-Baghdadi Proves Formidable Enemy," http://www.al-monitor.com/pulse/originals/2014/02/iraq-isis-baghdadi-mystery.html.

47. Middle East Monitor, "Corruption in the Palestinian Authority," https://www.middleeastmonitor.com/downloads/reports/20131214_CorruptioninthePalestinianAuthority.pdf.

48. Maggie O'Kane, "Where War is a Way of Life," http://www.theguardian.com/world/2001/oct/15/afghanistan.terrorism9.

49. Hannah Allam, "Records Show How Iraqi Extremists Withstood US Anti-terror Efforts," http://www.mcclatchydc.com/2014/06/23/231223/records-show-how-iraqi-extremists.html.

50. In fact, Moqtada al Sadr followed a similar blueprint in the Shiite suburbs of Baghdad in 2003, creating his own shell-state and social programs, and this approach proved very successful.

51. Aaron Zelin, "The Islamic State of Iraq and Syria Has a Consumer Protection Office," http://www.theatlantic.com/international/archive/2014/06/the-islamic-state-of-iraq-and-syria-has-a-consumer-protection-office/372769/.

52. Interview with Michael Przedlacki, September 16, 2014.

53. Fehim Taştekin, "Turkey's Syria borders an open door for smugglers," http://www.al-monitor.com/pulse/originals/2014/04/turkey-syria-borders-smuggling-guns-conflict-kurds-pkk-isis.html.

54. Aaron Zelin, "The Islamic State of Iraq and Syria Has a Consumer Protection Office." http://www.theatlantic.com/international/archive/2014/06/the-islamic-state-of-iraq-and-syria-has-a-consumer-protection-office/372769/.

55. Ibid.

56. Juan Foerom, "Rebel-Held Zone in Colombia Fears End of Truce." http://www.nytimes.com/2000/12/16/world/rebel-held-zone-in-colombia-fears-end-of-truce.html.

57. Jeremy Bowen, "Iraq Crisis: Fighting in Tikrit After 'Caliphate' Declared," http://www.bbc.com/news/world-middle-east-28092840.

58. Frank Gardner, "ISIS Rebels Declare 'Islamic State' in Iraq and Syria," http://www.bbc.co.uk/news/world-middle-east-28082962.

59. Francesca Borri, "Behind the Black Flag: Current, Former ISIL Fighters Speak," http://www.usnews.com/news/articles/2014/06/25/behind-the-black-flag-current-former-isil-fighters-speak.

60. William Dalrymple, "The ISIS Demand for a Caliphate Is About Power, Not Religion," http://www.theguardian.com/commentisfree/2014/jul/13/isis-caliphate-abu-bakr-al-baghdadi-jihadi-islam.

61. Dr. Zachariah Matthews, "The Golden Age of Islam," http://www.irfi.org/articles/articles_401_450/golden_age_of_islam.htm.

62. It would be a mistake, however, to include the Taliban regime in this category for several reasons, among them the importation of a foreign creed and political model into Afghanistan, a territory into which the caliphate had not originally reached.

63. Interview with an Albanian translator who worked for the US army in Kosovo, July 25, 2014.

64. Ludovica Iaccino, "ISIS Insurgents Tweet Picture of Beheaded Man: This is our ball. It's made of skin #WorldCup." http://www.ibtimes.co.uk/isis-insurgents -tweet-picture-beheaded-man-this-our-ball-its-made-skin-worldcup-1452643

65. Interview, Loretta Napoleoni.

66. Roula Khalaf, Sam Jones, "Selling Terror: How ISIS Details its Brutality," http://www.ft.com/cms/s/2/69e70954-f639-11e3-a038-00144feabdco.html.

67. BBC News, "Iraq's Annual Death Toll Highest in Five Years," http://www.bbc .com/news/world-middle-east-25568687.

68. Aaron Zelin, "The Islamic State of Iraq and Syria Has a Consumer Protection Office," http://www.theatlantic.com/international/archive/2014/06/the -islamic-state-of-iraq-and-syria-has-a-consumer-protection-office/372769/.

69. Francesca Borri, "Behind the Black Flag: Current, Former ISIL Fighters Speak," http://www.usnews.com/news/articles/2014/06/25/behind-the-black-flag -current-former-isil-fighters-speak.

70. Deborah Amos, "Islamic State Rule: Municipal Services and Public Beheadings," http://www.npr.org/blogs/parallels/2014/09/12/347748371/ islamic-state-rule-municipal-services-and-public-beheadings.

71. BBC News, "Battle for Iraq and Syria in Maps," http://www.bbc.co.uk/news/ world-middle-east-27838034.

72. Interview with Francesca Borri, September 15, 2014; *see also* Francesca Borri, *La Guerra Dentro* (Torino: Einaudi, 2014).

73. Michael Daly, "ISIS Leader: See You In New York." http://www.thedailybeast .com/articles/2014/06/14/isis-leader-see-you-in-new-york.html.

74. Fox News, "The Next Bin Laden: ISIS Leader Abu Bakr Al-Baghdadi," http:// foxnewsinsider.com/2014/06/13/next-bin-laden-isis-leader-abu-bakr-al-baghdadi.

75. Juan Sanchez, *Terrorism & Its Effects* (Global Media, 2007).

76. www.assabeel.net (n1 539, 2 May 2004).

77. Sohrab Ahmari, "Inside the Mind of the Western Jihadist," http://online.wsj .com/articles/sohrab-ahmari-inside-the-mind-of-the-western-jihadist-1409352541.

78. VICE News, "The Islamic State," https://www.youtube.com/watch?v=AUjHb4C7b94.

79. "Islamic State Switches to New Platforms After Twitter Block," http://www.bbc .com/news/world-middle-east-28843350.

80. Jack Healy, "For Jihad Recruits, a Pipeline from Minnesota to Militancy," http://www.nytimes.com/2014/09/07/us/for-Jihad-recruits-a-pipeline-from -Minnesota-to-militancy.html

81. J. M. Berger, "How ISIS Games Twitter," http://www.theatlantic.com/ international/archive/2014/06/isis-iraq-twitter-social-media-strategy/372856/.

82. Cahal Milmo, "ISIS Jihadists Using World Cup and Premiere League Hashtags to Promote Extremist Propaganda on Twitter," http://www.independent.co.uk/news/ world/middle-east/iraq-crisis-exclusive-isis-jihadists-using-world-cup-and-premier -league-hashtags-to-promote-extremist-propaganda-on-twitter-9555167.html.

83. "ISIS Leader al-Baghdadi Proves Formidable Enemy," http://www.al-monitor .com/pulse/originals/2014/02/iraq-isis-baghdadi-mystery.html.

84. Cahal Milmo, "ISIS Jihadists Using World Cup and Premiere League Hashtags to Promote Extremist Propaganda on Twitter," http://www.independent.co.uk/news/world/middle-east/iraq-crisis-exclusive-isis-jihadists-using-world-cup-and-premier-league-hashtags-to-promote-extremist-propaganda-on-twitter-9555167.html

85. Interview with Francesca Borri, September 15, 2014.

86. Sohrab Ahmari, "Inside the Mind of the Western Jihadist," http://online.wsj.com/articles/sohrab-ahmari-inside-the-mind-of-the-western-jihadist-1409352541.

87. Jonathan Owen, "British Fighters Make Up a Quarter of Foreign Jihadists," http://www.independent.co.uk/news/world/middle-east/islamic-state-backgrounder-british-fighters-make-up-a-quarter-of-foreign-jihadist-9681547.html.

88. Interview with Francesca Borri, September 15, 2014.

89. Jason Burke, "The ISIS Leader's Vision of the State is a Profoundly Contemporary One," http://www.theguardian.com/commentisfree/2014/aug/24/isis-abu-bakr-al-baghdadi-jason-burke.

90. Tom Englehardt, "Don't Walk Away From War: It's Not The American Way," http://original.antiwar.com/engelhardt/2014/06/10/dont-walk-away-from-war/

91. Robert Fisk, "Iraq Crisis: Sunni Caliphate Has Been Bankrolled by Saudi Arabia," http://www.belfasttelegraph.co.uk/opinion/columnists/robert-fisk/iraq-crisis-sunni-caliphate-has-been-bankrolled-by-saudi-arabia-30351679.html.

92. Damien McElroy, "ISIS Leader: Muslims Must Fight Until Rome Conquered," http://www.independent.ie/world-news/middle-east/isis-leader-muslims-must-fight-until-rome-conquered-30399749.html.

93. Ibid.

94. Saladin (1137/1138–March 4, 1193) was the first Sultan of Egypt and Syria and the founder of the Ayyubid dynasty. He led the Muslim opposition to the European Crusaders in the Levant. At the height of his power, his sultanate included Egypt, Syria, Mesopotamia, Hejaz, Yemen, and other parts of North Africa.

95. Because Qutb was imprisoned, tortured, and eventually hanged by the Nasser regime, his suffering has become emblematic of the victims of repressive Arab regimes.

96. McElroy, "ISIS Leader: Muslims Must Fight Until Rome Conquered."

97. Ben Hubbard, "ISIS Threatens Al Qaeda as Flagship Movement of Extremists," http://www.nytimes.com/2014/07/01/world/middleeast/isis-threatens-al-qaeda-as-flagship-movement-of-extremists.html.

98. "How Saudi Arabia helped Isis take over the north of Iraq," http://www.belfasttelegraph.co.uk/opinion/how-saudi-arabia-helped-isis-take-over-the-north-of-iraq-30435038.html.

99. Nick Patton Walsh, "The Secret Jihadi Smuggling Route Through Turkey," http://www.cnn.com/2013/11/04/world/europe/isis-gaining-strength-on-syria-turkey-border/.

100. "Under the Microscope," Al Jazeera Arabic Satellite TV broadcast, July 1, 2004, broadcast (in Arabic).

101. Various, "The Biography of Sheikh Abu al-Baghdadi," https://archive.org/stream/TheBiographyOfSheikhAbuBakrAlBaghdadi/The%20biography%20of%20Sheikh%20Abu%20Bakr%20Al-Baghdadi_djvu.txt.

102. Albert Hourani, *A History of the Arab Peoples (Cambridge, MA:* Harvard University Press, 2003).

103. http://www.oxfordislamicstudies.com/article/opr/t125/e2356.

104. Ibid.

105. "The Future of Sharia: Negotiating Islam in the Context of the Secular State," http://sharia.law.emory.edu/index.html%3Fq=en%252Fwars_apostasy.html.

106. "How Saudi Arabia helped Isis take over the north of Iraq," http://www.belfasttelegraph.co.uk/opinion/how-saudi-arabia-helped-isis-take-over-the-north-of-iraq-30435038.html.

107. Mike Schuster, "The Origins of the Shiite-Sunni Split," http://www.npr.org/blogs/parallels/2007/02/12/7332087/the-origins-of-the-shiite-sunni-split.

108. "The Saud Family and Wahhabi Islam," http://countrystudies.us/saudi-arabia/7.htm.

109. Nassima Neggaz, "The Falls of Baghdad in 1258 and 2003: A Study in Sunni-Shi'i Clashing Memories," https://repository.library.georgetown.edu/handle/10822/707405.

110. *Bashaer*, no. 26, December 27, 2004. For more information on the concept of Americans as the new Mongols see also "Iraqi Vice President: 'Thousands of Suicide Attackers Will Fight Against US,'" *Der Spiegel*, February 1, 2003; Sam Hamod, "The New Mongols," *al Jazeera*, November 19, 2004.

111. Ibid.

112. On April 28, 2003 Saddam Hussein declared that Bush had entered Baghdad with the help of Alqami; see *al Quds al Arabi*, April 30, 2003.

113. Loretta Napoleoni, "The Myth of Zarqawi," http://www.antiwar.com/orig/napoleoni.php?articleid=7988.

114. Back in 2003, the presence of foreign fighters and of suicide bombers in the Sunni Triangle was one of the key elements that differentiated the Sunni resistance from the Shiite insurgency. Another was the backgrounds and motivations of the two groups. While the latter was essentially a class struggle, the former was a counter-Crusade against Coalition forces and a civil war against the Shias. From the outset, Moqtada al Sadr's Shiite revolt had sought political recognition for his followers, theretofore excluded from key political positions, and a share of the political pie for al Sadr himself. Indeed, the Shias managed to attain full control of a "democratic Iraq;" Sunni insurgents, instead, were busy fighting a full-fledged war against occupying powers and, after the suicide attack against the Imam Ali Mosque, a civil war against Muslim heretics.

115. John Cantlie, "Lend Me Your Ears," https://www.youtube.com/watch?v=Vcew3qmidRI.

116. Ali Khedery, "How ISIS Came to Be," http://www.theguardian.com/world/2014/aug/22/syria-iraq-incubators-isis-jihad.

117. Ibid.

118. Ibid.

119. Ibid.

120. Amnesty International, "Nigeria: Gruesome footage implicates military in war crimes," http://www.amnesty.org/en/news/nigeria-gruesome-footage-implicates-military-war-crimes-2014-08-05.

121. Mary Kaldor, *New and Old Wars: Organized Violence in a Global Era* (Malden, MA: Polity Press, 1999).